Making and Tinkering With STEM

Solving Design Challenges With Young Children

Cate Heroman

National Association for the Education of Young Children
Washington, DC

National Association for the
Education of Young Children
1313 L Street NW, Suite 500
Washington, DC 20005-4101
202-232-8777 • 800-424-2460
NAEYC.org

NAEYC Books

Senior Director, Content Strategy
and Development
Susan Friedman

Editor-in-Chief
Kathy Charner

Senior Creative Design Manager
Audra Meckstroth

Senior Editor
Holly Bohart

Creative Design Specialist
Charity Coleman

Associate Editor
Rossella Procopio

Through its publications program,
the National Association for the
Education of Young Children
(NAEYC) provides a forum for
discussion of major issues and ideas
in the early childhood field, with
the hope of provoking thought and
promoting professional growth. The
views expressed or implied in this
book are not necessarily those of
the Association.

Permissions

The figure and text on page 4 are adapted, with permission, from *Tinker Kit: Educators' Guide*, Boston Children's Museum.

Photo Credits

Copyright © NAEYC: 22 (top and middle), 24, 34 (both), 36, 42 (both), 58 (both), 60, 62, 70 (left and middle), 72, 74 (all), 76, 90 (both), 96, 110 (middle), 114, and 124 (both)

Copyright © iStock: iv, 1, 3, 13, 14, 16, 22 (bottom), 38 (left), 52, 66 (both), and 112

Courtesy of Jamey Firnberg, Rockit Surgery: 22 (glue gun) and 137

Courtesy of Cate Heroman: 2, 9, 11 (all), 12 (all), 17, 19, 30 (all), 32, 38 (right), 44, 46 (both), 48, 50 (bottom), 54 (bottom), 56, 64, 70 (right), 80, 82 (all), 86 (both), 88, 98 (both), 100, 102 (both), 104, 106 (all), 108, 118 (both), and 120

Courtesy of Ryan Moreno, REM Learning Center: 21 (right), 84, and 125

Courtesy of Ann Scalley, Lesley Ellis School: 26 (all), 28, 38 (middle), 40, 68, 78, 92, and 94 (top)

Courtesy of Kerry Sheldon, Louisiana State University Early Childhood Education Laboratory Preschool: 21 (left) and 54 (top)

Courtesy of Sarah West, Louisiana State University Early Childhood Education Laboratory Preschool: 6 (both), 7, 8, 20 (bottom), 94 (bottom), and 110 (left and right)

Courtesy of Paige Zittrauer, Louisiana State University Laboratory School: 50 (top) and 116

Disclaimer

Neither the publisher nor the author can be held responsible for any damage or injury incurred while implementing the activities described in this book. Please exercise appropriate and reasonable supervision at all times based on your comfort level and the age and capability of each child.

Library of Congress Control Number: 2016955248

ISBN: 978-1-938113-28-4

Item 1130

Table of Contents

What You Need to Know About Tinkering, Making, and Engineering

Think back to your earliest memories of making something, tinkering, or inventing something to solve a problem. What did you do? Did you

- Figure out an easier way to lift things into a tree house?

- Tape boxes together to create a cool car?

- Build an elaborate fort?

- Use sticks, leaves, or pine needles to create a floor plan for a dream house?

- Roll toy cars down ramps and adjust the ramps to make the cars go faster?

- Fold and refold paper airplanes so they fly farther?

- Take apart an old toy and try to put it back together?

How much time did you spend thinking about and doing these activities? Where did the materials come from? Did you return to your ideas over many days and try to improve them and make them better? How did you feel when you solved the problem?

This is what tinkering, making, and engineering look like in early childhood. Children initially use their senses to explore the physical properties of materials. They tinker as they take things apart, put things together, figure out how things work, and attempt to build and make creations using tools. When they are faced with a problem, children ask questions, make plans, work together, test their ideas, solve problems, improve their ideas to make them better, and share their ideas and creations with others. These are the thinking processes and actions that scientists and engineers use. These professionals, when faced with a challenge, solve real-world problems that often come with constraints, including limited materials, time, and funds to develop solutions.

Design Challenges: Where Story Characters' Problems Meet the Real World

In this book, you will find tinkering, making, and engineering challenges appropriate for 3- to 8-year-old children that build a strong foundation for future learning in the STEM fields (science, technology, engineering, and mathematics). These experiences begin at a familiar starting place—the problems characters in picture books face. The problem might be a troll who stands between the three billy goats and the green grass they want to eat on the other side of the bridge, a child who is afraid to go to the zoo, or a boat that sinks a little lower into the sea each time an animal steps aboard. After reading a book together, you might use challenges such as these as prompts to extend children's thinking and problem-solving skills by inviting them to

- Construct a new bridge for the three billy goats to avoid the nasty troll

- Design an animal mask or costume to help the child who is afraid of animals conquer her fear

- Build a boat that floats and holds pennies or other objects

The design challenges offer ways to integrate early literacy with all areas of development (social and emotional, physical, and cognitive) and content-area learning (mathematics, science, social studies, the arts, and technology). Each begins with an invitation to tinker with and explore materials and tools ("Tinker With the Materials"). Through this tinkering, children figure out how materials and tools work, how to take things apart, and how to put things together. They also develop their fine motor skills. Tinkering takes time. It involves the process of *iteration*—when something doesn't work, children are encouraged to try another strategy or use different materials or tools.

Next, the challenges provide a prompt ("Making") to make something that will help the character in the story solve the problem. For example, children use the materials available to them, along with their creativity and imagination, to make a squirrel-proof birdfeeder or a tall, beautiful building like one in their community.

To add complexity, each experience includes an engineering challenge ("Engineering"). These engineering tasks include constraints or requirements to consider while using the same process as engineers. For instance, for the story *Goldilocks and the Three Bears,* an engineering challenge would be to build a chair that doesn't wobble and can hold a five-pound weight.

In general, the design challenges are most appropriate for children in preschool through third grade and have the flexibility to be used with diverse learners. The challenges have a "low threshold, high ceiling, and wide walls" (see Resnick 2005). A low threshold, or floor, means that there is an easy way to get started. Very young children will spend a great deal of time exploring the properties of materials and tools before they actually make something. A high ceiling indicates that there are many ways you can expand these challenges. Slight adjustments can make them more challenging or complex. Wide walls enable children to take many different pathways to explore the design challenges as well as integrate curriculum from other learning domains. Rather than restrict children to just a few materials selected by you, offer them a wide variety of choices to solve the problem. Each challenge includes a section called "Going Deeper" with suggestions for making the challenge more complex or encouraging children to solve problems in a different way. Use your understanding of the children's knowledge, skills, and abilities to adjust each challenge to meet the needs of the group as well as of individuals.

With a strong emphasis on STEM, these challenges enable children to apply skills in math and science in a way that is meaningful and engaging. They provide opportunities for using and strengthening important executive function skills, such as planning, focusing attention, organizing information, persisting, thinking flexibly, and solving problems. Taken together, these skills are important in school and in life. Implementing these challenges helps prepare children to solve the problems of the future.

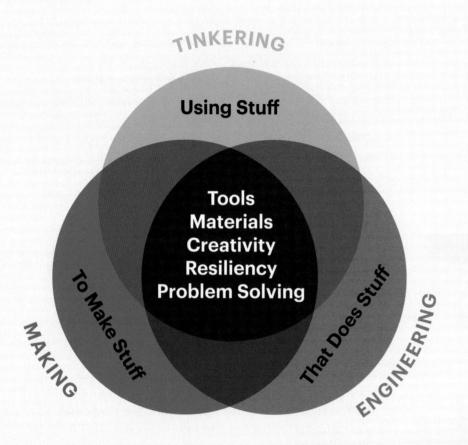

Tinkering is the playful relative of the more serious activity of engineering. Engineering starts with a problem to be solved: "We need a bridge" or "We need a house to live in." Tinkering starts with much simpler questions: "What can I do with this?" or "How does this work?"

And then there is the term *making*. Tinkering and making are often used interchangeably, but making lies somewhere in between tinkering and engineering.

Tinkering is using stuff.

Making is using stuff to make stuff (that sometimes does stuff, but sometimes is just cool).

Engineering is using stuff to make stuff that does stuff.

When children tinker, they are learning about the properties of materials and the capabilities of tools. They are developing their fine motor skills as well. Tinkering often leads to making something, and it is absolutely the foundation to more complex making, technology, and engineering. Learning how to manipulate tools, understand the properties of materials, and identify unique solutions to problems is at the core of all of making and engineering. And helping children develop these skills through tinkering is the best place to start.

Adapted, by permission, from Boston Children's Museum, *Tinker Kit: Educators' Guide* (Boston: Boston Children's Museum, 2016), 4.

Is It Tinkering, Making, or Engineering?

Design challenges connect with the increased interest in early STEM education. What are tinkering, making, and design engineering? How are they the same or different? The Boston Children's Museum (2016) offers an excellent explanation, as seen on page 4.

This book includes all three aspects of maker education—tinkering, making, and engineering. All three are valuable experiences in early STEM education. The skills and dispositions children learn and acquire during making and tinkering become an important part of the engineering design process.

Developing Skills for Design Challenges

During everyday experiences in the classroom, you can help children develop skills they will later use to solve design challenges. These skills include

- Asking questions
- Formulating plans
- Making observational drawings
- Measuring and recording findings
- Evaluating outcomes

- Creating diagrams
- Using art and construction materials (e.g., wire, tape, clay, scissors, cardboard)
- Handling real tools (e.g., screwdrivers, low-temperature glue guns, timers)

Find opportunities to incorporate these skills in your daily activities, especially during tinkering and making experiences. The more time children have to practice these skills day in and day out, the more comfortable and confident they will feel in applying them during the design challenge activities. They will already be familiar with the tools, materials, and processes needed to solve problems.

Tinkering and Making Experiences

Tinkering is an important element of the maker movement that is sweeping the country in schools, libraries, makerspaces, and museums. This movement is driven by people's desire to create something with their hands. The concept is certainly not new to early childhood.

> What is a *makerspace?* It's a place where people gather to tinker, make things, invent, create, explore, and make discoveries using a wide variety of real tools and materials.

Children engaged in open-ended tinkering and making experiences practice skills they will use throughout their lifetime. The end product of tinkering and making experiences is not as important as the process. As children grow and mature, their ability to use tools, collaborate with others, experiment, observe, make discoveries, tap into prior knowledge, communicate, and persevere will continue to develop and flourish.

Children love to take things apart—a process known as *deconstruction*. When children take things apart, they see how the parts work together and gain insight into how to put components together in ways that create something new (see the vignette to the right). Old, small appliances (with cords removed), a computer and keyboard, and broken mechanical toys are all ideal for taking apart. Provide child-size, real tools such as screwdrivers and pliers. After children take apart the objects and investigate them, sort the parts and save them for repurposing and reusing. For example, children might create a self-portrait or a picture by using a low-temperature glue gun to attach computer keys and other loose parts onto a piece of cardboard.

A first grade teacher finds a battery-operated plush dog at a garage sale and decides to use it in a take-apart activity. In a small group experience, the children closely observe the dog and dictate everything they notice as the teacher records their words. They learn that they can make the dog bark without turning it on by pushing its head back and forth. Next, they guess what they might find inside by feeling the toy and then draw their predictions. One child feels a spring in the tail. Another child thinks there might be a battery in the leg. The children use scissors to remove the dog's fur. There are squeals of excitement as they confirm their predictions: "Look, I was right! There *is* a spring in the tail!" After they remove the fur, they turn on the switch to watch the dog move again.

At the base of the head, they discover a small wedge-shaped part covered with tissue paper with a small cone attached. It seems to have a spring inside and is the piece that causes the dog to bark. The children cut the tissue paper covering the wedge and discover that the dog no longer barks when they push its head. Much time is spent investigating this tiny piece, and the children decide that the air pushed out of the cone made the barking sound. To test their hypothesis, they cover the piece with some tissue paper and tape, and the dog barks again!

They continue using small screwdrivers to remove the plastic and discover a small motor and gears.

The parts are harvested and sorted for future use. The teacher later mounts the parts to a block of wood and shows children how to use alligator clips to connect it to a battery pack. The mounted mechanical parts and battery pack are placed in the science area for the children to observe the mechanical motions again and again.

The design challenges in this book include a prompt to make or build something—a kind of prototype—as a way for children to represent their ideas and thinking in response to the problem in the story. For example, after listening to the story of *Iggy Peck, Architect,* the children are invited to build a tall building using the materials and tools available.

Engineering Experiences

Each experience in this book also includes an engineering design challenge, which is open ended and requires children to work collaboratively to generate ideas and solve problems. Each engineering challenge describes some limitations or criteria to determine if a solution is successful. For example, children may be asked to design a pet carrier that is strong enough to carry a five-pound pet and other pet care items. Some of the engineering tasks require more advanced reasoning and skills in science and math. Use your knowledge of each child to determine the appropriateness of the challenges for individuals and groups.

Engineers solve problems by making things that work or by making things work better. They follow a series of steps when they investigate a problem and try to come up with a solution. There are many variations on this model, but the basic steps are these:

- **Think about it.** What is the problem? Brainstorm ideas. What materials do you have or need? Make a plan. Draw or sketch your ideas.

- **Build or create it.** Gather the materials you need and build or create the solution you came up with.

- **Try it.** Test your creation.

- **Revise or make it better.** What works and what doesn't? How could you change it to make it better? Try it again.

- **Share.** Show someone else your creation. Talk about how you made it. Listen to their ideas about how they might improve it.

Young children might not follow these steps in a linear fashion. They might start at any point, go back and forth between steps, or spend more time on one step than another.

To help children think like engineers, use problems that happen during daily classroom experiences and apply the engineering design process to help them find solutions. This is what Kerry did in her classroom:

> In Kerry's classroom of 3- and 4-year-olds, a child drops a small metal car in the space between

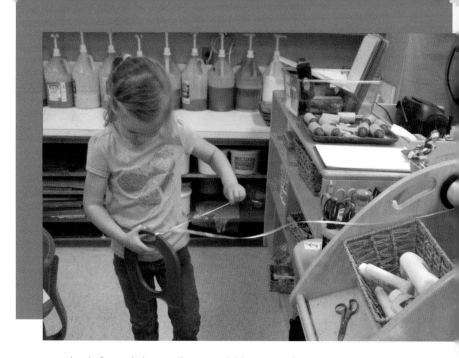

the loft and the wall. It would be easy for Kerry to retrieve the car, but she uses this as a real-world problem for the children to solve. During a class meeting, they discuss the problem and come up with possible solutions. Kerry gathers the materials that the children suggest, and during choice time they invent contraptions that can be used to get the car. Each child works with a partner to test their device. If it doesn't work, they talk about why and what they might change to make it better. After persisting, they figure out a way to retrieve the car by suspending a magnet on the end of a string. Kerry documents the experience with pictures. The group debriefs during a class meeting, and the children dictate a story about the experience to share with families and visitors.

The Learning Environment

The ultimate goal behind the design challenges is to help children think creatively, take risks, and solve problems. Just as engineers solve problems everywhere, children tackling these design challenges can work on them in any area of the classroom as well as outdoors. Problem solving occurs wherever children are.

A flexible room arrangement is key for tinkering, making, and engineering challenges. Read the challenge and then consider your space needs. Some challenges may occur at a table with one or two children, while others might require rearranging the furniture to accommodate larger projects and more children.

Some teachers with larger classrooms set up a dedicated space for making and tinkering. These areas typically have a shelf for storing and displaying materials and tools, a power source, and a large table.

The materials used in the design challenges are typically found in the art area or in the science area of the classroom. If your classroom is not large enough to accommodate a dedicated makerspace, use these areas for storing materials. Positioning these two areas in close proximity to each other helps children access the tools and materials more easily. What is most important is that children know where to find the materials they need to accomplish a task. As you observe children working on a challenge, you might suggest and help them locate a material that is not on display but that would be helpful in solving the problem.

Children need lots of open-ended materials and loose parts for tinkering, making, and engineering experiences. Organize and attractively display these materials so children are encouraged to use their imagination to invent ways to use them.

Gathering Materials

Most materials suggested in this book are found in your classroom. Other sources for materials might be

- Donations from families or local businesses
- Local reusable resource centers (www.reuseresources.org/find-a-center.html)
- Garage sales or thrift stores

To encourage families to donate materials, place a container or bin in a convenient location. Family members can drop off their items when they come to pick up or drop off their children. Be specific about what you want, and ask that any recyclables be clean. Identify items that you cannot accept because of safety or storage concerns.

On the following page is one teacher's wish list for a makerspace area. She used these materials for making, tinkering, and engineering design challenges.

Examples of Materials for Tinkering, Making, and Engineering

Basic equipment and tools	Child-size safety goggles, low-temperature glue guns, child-safe cardboard cutters, measuring tapes, rulers, paintbrushes, scissors, tweezers, magnifying glasses, flashlights, funnels, clipboards, staplers, unbreakable mirrors, egg timers, eyedroppers, funnels, measuring cups, trays, magnets, balance scales, balls, marbles, PVC pipe parts, pulleys, ice trays, child-size hammers, pliers, screwdrivers
Consumables	*Things to build with:* craft sticks, toothpicks, cardboard tubes, drinking straws, new Styrofoam trays, cardboard, pipe cleaners, wheels, wood scraps, wooden spools, plastic cups, paper plates, chopsticks or wooden skewers, corks *Things to use to connect:* tape (masking, duct, cellophane, electrical, paper), staples and staplers, glue, glue sticks, brads, string, yarn, twine, wire, cardboard connectors (e.g., Mr. McGroovy's box rivets, www.mrmcgroovys.com), adhesive Velcro, binder clips, clothespins, rubber bands *Things to sculpt and mold:* clay, Plasticine, playdough, modeling tools (e.g., rolling pins, scrapers) *Things for mixing and chemistry explorations:* unbreakable cups, bowls, pitchers, beakers, and test tubes; spoons; coffee filters; food coloring; various ingredients (e.g., vinegar, baking soda, yeast); balloons; ingredients (e.g., white glue, cornstarch) for making polymers such as gak, silly putty, or oobleck *Things to use for decoration:* pom-poms, feathers, googly eyes, stickers, glitter, fun foam, beads *Things to use with fabrics and textiles:* thread, yarn, dull darning needles, plastic mesh canvas, weaving looms, fabric markers, buttons, thread, embroidery floss, felt *Things to use for writing and drawing:* pencils, crayons, markers, colored pencils, pens, individual white boards, paper
Electronics and technology	Batteries, battery holders, small hobby motors, flashlight bulbs, LEDs, finger lights, kits for beginning circuitry, on/off switches, buzzers

You don't need all of these materials to get started! The key is to start small. Collect the materials you need for a particular design challenge, and the children will learn how to use those materials and might incorporate them in a different way during another challenge. Your collection of materials will grow over time as you try new challenges. The appendix of this book contains a comprehensive list of the design challenges, children's books, and suggested materials.

Organizing and Displaying Materials

When materials are organized and displayed attractively, children can clearly see possibilities for using them. For example, they may look at all the choices available to decide how to connect a craft stick to a clothespin. If one

strategy doesn't work, they can return to the materials to find something else.

They also learn that everything has a place and that this makes both finding things and cleaning up easier. Clear plastic containers or baskets are ideal for storing materials. Place materials at children's eye level.

One way to present materials is through the use of tinkering trays. Tinkering trays invite children to create and invent, and they promote independence and decision making. Shallow containers divided into sections, such as a shadow box, drawer, cutlery tray, muffin tin, egg carton, or drawer organizer, are ideal for creating a tinkering tray. Fill the sections with small, open-ended objects or loose parts for use in building or creating. Place the tray in the

center of the table so all children can see what is available and reach what they need. Restock or swap out materials as needed. Tinkering trays can be used not only with design challenges but also in general making and tinkering activities. When you introduce the tinkering tray, put some simple rules in place, such as take only what you need, keep the tray in the center of the table, or let an adult move the tinkering tray. Show the children that each material has a special place, and demonstrate how to return the materials to their homes.

Showcase children's finished creations so others can benefit from the learning involved. Such displays encourage children to talk about the process they used and inspire others to make their own creations. Sometimes a project may take days to complete. Designate a shelf or other space for "works in progress" so children can come back to their ideas and continue refining them over time.

Safety

Keeping children safe while using real tools involves letting them take and manage risks. Using real tools is very empowering to young children and promotes a sense of independence because it communicates that you trust them. As a teacher, your role is to clearly teach children how to use the tools safely and monitor their use. For example, establish rules for the use of a low-temperature glue gun with a protective tip and show children how to place the glue gun in a cookie tin when it is not in use. If you notice a safety risk, point it out and use it as an opportunity to teach safe handling techniques.

it out, and if it does not work they try something else. Use their failed attempts as opportunities to help them learn and grow as well as to develop perseverance.

The challenges presented in this book can be used flexibly. They are not in a particular order. Choose one that relates to the interests of one or more of the children in your group, what is happening in your school or community, or what your class is currently learning about. For instance, the design challenge "Help! It's Stuck!" (page 54) would be a natural fit for Kerry's class to use after they discovered the toy car that was stuck (see page 8).

Here's the big picture of the design challenge process:

Before

1. Review one of the design challenges in this book.

2. Select the picture book (or alternate selection) you plan to read. If you choose an alternate book, you may need to adjust the challenge a bit.

3. Gather the materials and other items you think might be useful. Many materials will already be in your classroom, but you may need to find additional items for a particular challenge.

4. Introduce new materials and tools. As you gradually add new materials and tools, teach children how to use them safely and where to store them. Brainstorm possibilities of how the materials or tools might be used. Put the new materials and tools out for open-ended exploration prior to introducing the challenge.

Introducing Design Challenges

Depending on your schedule and the time available, you may wish to work on a single design challenge over several days. You may choose to read a book one day and the next day introduce the design challenge by helping children recall the problem the character faced. Tinkering and solving problems take time. Engineers make prototypes or models and then go through several versions to find the best solution, and the same is true for children as they work on design challenges. They create a solution and test

5. Display the materials attractively. For challenges that can be worked on at a table, display the materials in baskets or in clear containers on a shelf close by. You may also place a tinkering tray in the center of the table for easy access. For larger projects requiring more space, place a cart with organized materials and tools in the making area. Display the book used in the challenge for easy reference.

During

6. Read the story to the children.

7. Discuss the story with the children. What is the problem in the story? Relate the problem to children's prior experiences—for example, "Have you ever built something that would fly or roll or move in some other way, but then it didn't do what you wanted it to?"

8. Together, brainstorm other ways the character in the book might solve the problem.

9. Present the challenge. You might read the book one day and introduce the challenge on another. For younger children or children who are learning how to approach design challenges, use the tinkering and making suggestions. For older children or those with the skills necessary to complete the task, add the engineering

challenges. Discuss ideas about what materials or tools they might use. Adjust the challenges to meet the needs and abilities of the individual children in your class.

10. Invite children to make a plan. What materials will they need to carry out their plan? What will their design look like? Have them draw or sketch their ideas and label the parts. Drawing offers a powerful way for children (and adults) to represent their ideas, clarify their thinking, and communicate their ideas to others.

11. Support children as they build their constructions. Observe closely and try to understand what and

how they are thinking. Talk about what you notice. Encourage them to describe what they are doing, and expand on their language. For example, if a child says her building won't stay still, say, "Hmm, your building is too wobbly. What can we do to make it more stable?" Resist the temptation to give too much information or make suggestions too quickly. Let children struggle with the problem a bit. When something doesn't work, use it as an opportunity to discuss what might work better and why. Be available to help children locate the materials they want and need.

12. Ask open-ended questions and offer thought-provoking statements to stimulate children's thinking. It is important to base your questions and comments on what you are observing. Failure to do so disrupts a child's thinking and may lead him to ignore your question or abandon the activity. Here are some questions and prompts to consider:

» What do you think will happen if _____?

» What can you do to make your structure more stable?

» How can you make the ball roll all the way through the maze?

» What did you notice about _____?

» Tell me about _____.

» How can you make it stronger?

» What tools could you use to _____?

» What did you think about when you designed your _____?

» How could you change your design so that it _____?

» What other way could you use these things?

» How could you make this go faster? slower?

» I wonder why your invention keeps falling over.

13. If a child is frustrated or stuck, offer some possible solutions to try. Give some hints and help the child brainstorm possibilities.

14. Invite children to try their solutions. Have them think about and discuss what happened. Did their solution work? If it did, what did the children learn? If it didn't, what could they change so it does work? How could they improve it or make it better?

15. Use the "Going Deeper" option to scaffold children's learning and offer them additional challenges. You might suggest a different material or strategy; adjust or add requirements of weight, height, length, or volume; or specify something different that you want their construction to do.

After

16. Give children opportunities to share their work with others. Invite them to reflect on what they learned by explaining their creation to another person, writing a story, acting out the experience, writing a song, drawing a picture, creating a graph,

or any other way that is meaningful to them. For challenges that particularly engage the children's interest, consider inviting family members, program administrators, other classes, and community partners to your class to see and hear about what the children have created. This gives children the opportunity to express their ideas, share their processes, and answer questions. Sharing their work also helps you understand what the children learned and how to advocate for early STEM learning by demonstrating what it looks like.

One way children can "go deeper" is by adding motion to something they create using cardboard linkages and automata. *Linkages* are important parts of machines and tools such as pliers, folding dryer racks, folding baby carriages, scissor lifts, scissors, and locomotive wheels. A linkage consists of a lever and a joint or fulcrum. Cardboard linkages provide a way of figuring out how to make things move and then constructing mechanical toys from cardboard strips and brass brads.

Automata, sometimes referred to as mechanical toys or kinetic art, use mechanical elements such as cams (wheels) and cranks to make the parts of a sculpture or machine move. To learn more about linkages and automata, investigate some of the many online sites that describe and illustrate them.

Using High-Tech Materials and Equipment

Do you like to learn to use new and exciting technologies? Do you have access to tools, materials, and equipment that you might consider high-tech? If so, then think about ways to integrate these new technologies into design challenges in a meaningful way. You may have a STEM lab, makerspace, or a "fab lab" with high-tech materials in your school or community. Or you may have a parent or contact in the community who could come to your classroom as an expert to demonstrate a new tool or show your class a new technique or technology. Reach out to others who might assist if you want to learn more. Take time to tinker and play to figure out how things work.

Offering children opportunities to tinker with simple circuits is an example of a skill that can be used to add enhancements to their project. Once they know how to create a simple circuit, they may use LEDs, copper tape, and batteries to add lights to a building made of boxes. The design challenges offer a way for children, with the help of an adult or older student, to use electronics in a purposeful, meaningful way:

- Add lights by creating simple circuits with LEDs and batteries

- Make things move by adding batteries and small hobby motors

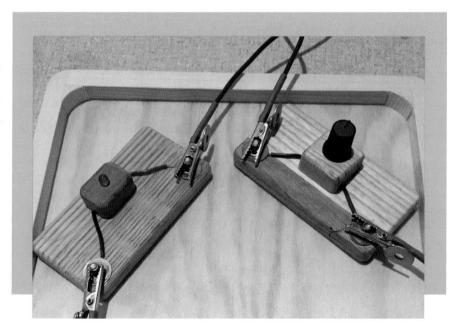

- Add sound, alarms, and sensors

- Create a stop-motion animation or digital storytelling to share with others

- Make props and pieces using high-tech equipment like 3-D printers or laser cutters typically found in makerspaces and libraries

- Integrate robotics with a project

Involving Families

Family members can play a meaningful role in the implementation of engineering design challenges in your classroom. They can

- Help you locate and gather resources

- Translate stories in home languages, if needed

- Assist children during the design process

- Serve as an expert resource person for your class

- Demonstrate a skill or how to use a tool

- Be an audience for children to share their ideas and processes

Use your newsletter or other communication methods to let families know that you would like them to be involved, and offer a number of ways for them to do so. Also share ideas for ways they can extend their children's learning at home. Tap into families' interests and find out what they like to do together.

What Children Can Learn as They Work on Design Challenges

	Social and Emotional	Physical	Cognitive
DEVELOPMENT	· Working well with others · Sharing · Respecting the rights and work of others · Regulating emotions · Following directions	· Fine motor skills—use of hands, dexterity, eye-hand coordination · Gross motor skills—balance, stability, traveling, manipulating balls or similar objects	· Problem solving · Reasoning · Creativeness and inventiveness · Flexible thinking · Logical thinking · Persistence

	Language and Literacy	Math	Science and Engineering
CONTENT LEARNING	· Listening comprehension · Expressing oneself · Vocabulary · Comprehension of story	· Numeracy · Comparing and measuring · Using data · Geometry and spatial sense · Patterns	· Observing and making predictions · Scientific inquiry · Physical science · Life science · Earth and the environment · Engineering
	Social Studies	The Arts	Technology
	· Jobs in the community · Economics · How people live	· Visual arts (painting, drawing, sketching, modeling, sculpting, building, weaving, etc.)	· Tool use · Basic technology skills · How people use technology

Observing and Assessing Children's Learning

As you implement design challenges, you will find rich opportunities for documenting what children know and can do. Take photos and videos, collect work samples, and record what children say. Link their learning to your program goals. The chart on page 18 provides examples of some knowledge, skills, and dispositions that you might document during the process.

The design challenges that follow are intended to inspire a mindset for tinkering, making, and engineering. As children identify problems, make plans, build and create, test their ideas, revise their plans or make them better, and share their creations with others, they are learning skills that they will apply throughout life. Use these challenges as a starting point for supporting STEM-rich play and inquiry that will make teaching and learning in your classroom interesting and exciting. And when you are ready to move beyond the challenges presented here, use the "Design Challenge Planning Template" in the appendix to plan additional challenges that will be equally engaging for children.

References

Boston Children's Museum. 2016. *Tinker Kit: Educators' Guide*. Boston: Boston Children's Museum. www.bostonchildrensmuseum.org/sites/default/files/pdfs/Tinker_Kit_Educators_Guide_singles_web.pdf.

Resnick, M., B. Myers, K. Nakakoji, B. Shneiderman, R. Pausch, T. Selker, & M. Eisenberg. 2005. "Design Principles for Tools to Support Creative Thinking." www.cs.umd.edu/hcil/CST/Papers/designprinciples.htm.

Design Challenges

Baby Bear's Chair

Inspired by *Goldilocks and the Three Bears*
by Caralyn Buehner, illustrated by Mark Buehner

Baby Bear's Chair

LET'S LOOK AT THE PROBLEM

After a walk in the woods, the three bears return to their house to find Little Wee Bear's chair broken, his porridge gone, and someone sleeping in his bed.

What do the three bears do about the broken chair? How do you think they could have fixed it? Have you ever fixed something that broke at home or at school? How did you do it?

MATERIALS

- ☐ Reusable resources such as boxes, cardboard sheets and tubes, wood scraps, and craft sticks
- ☐ Connectors such as tape, glue, a low-temperature glue gun, cardboard connectors, and brads
- ☐ Tools such as scissors, child-safe cardboard cutters, and measuring tapes
- ☐ Broken or nonworking items such as toys or small appliances
- ☐ A balance scale and a 5 lb. weight
- ☐ Paper and markers, crayons, or pencils

Safety note: Adult assistance needed in cutting cardboard

TINKER WITH THE MATERIALS

Pretend you work at a fix-it shop near the woods where Goldilocks might take Little Wee Bear's chair to be repaired. Look at the broken things (toys and small appliances) and at the tools and materials you might use to fix them. What can you fix? Try some different connectors to hold things together. Which one seems to work best with the object you chose to fix?

STEM CONCEPTS

balance / design engineering / force / gravity / measurement / number concepts / patterning / scientific inquiry / stability

Baby Bear's Chair

THE DESIGN CHALLENGE

Making Build a chair that stands on its own.

Engineering Build a stable chair that doesn't wobble and can hold an object that weighs at least five pounds.

WORKING ON THE DESIGN CHALLENGE

- **Think about it.** How will you build the chair? What does your chair need to include? What will you do to make it stable? Draw or sketch your ideas.

    Engineering. What part of Little Wee Bear's chair do you think broke and why? What part of the chair does he sit on? What part keeps him off the floor? How can you use this information to design your chair? How will you make the chair strong so Goldilocks can't break it?

- **Build or create it.** Gather your materials to build the chair. Make sure that it is strong and sturdy.

- **Try it.** Try to make the chair stand up on its own.

    Engineering. What will you use for a five-pound weight? What is the most weight the chair will hold?

- **Revise or make it better.** Does it work? If it doesn't, what can you change to make the chair better, stronger, or more stable?

    Engineering. Is your chair stable (no wobbling)? Does it hold at least five pounds?

- **Share.** Tell someone about your chair and how you made it. Ask them if they have ideas about how to make it better.

    Engineering. Test several chairs. Which one holds the most weight? Look closely at that chair and discuss with someone which features you think make it strong.

Baby Bear's Chair

QUESTIONS AND COMMENTS

What do you think will happen if _____?

Tell me about your chair.

How much weight do you think your chair will hold?

What part do you think is the weakest? How could you strengthen that part?

BACK TO THE PROBLEM IN THE BOOK

Why do you think Little Wee Bear's chair breaks but the other chairs do not?

How do you think your chair compares with Little Wee Bear's chair?

GOING DEEPER

- Design a chair that reclines. What other tools and materials would you need? How would you make it?

- Use tools to take apart and/or fix a broken chair donated by a family, friend, school, or community member. What can you do to make it usable and look new again?

- What if animals could sit in chairs? How would you design and make a chair for a snake? a giraffe? a porcupine? an octopus? an ant?

- Examine different types of wheelchairs. How do they work? Interview someone who uses a wheelchair. What are their ideas for making it better? Design and make a prototype (model) of a wheelchair that helps a person do a special task or an activity.

OTHER BOOKS TO USE

A Chair for Baby Bear / Kaye Umansky, illustrated by Chris Fisher

A Chair for My Mother / Vera B. Williams

Peter's Chair / Ezra Jack Keats

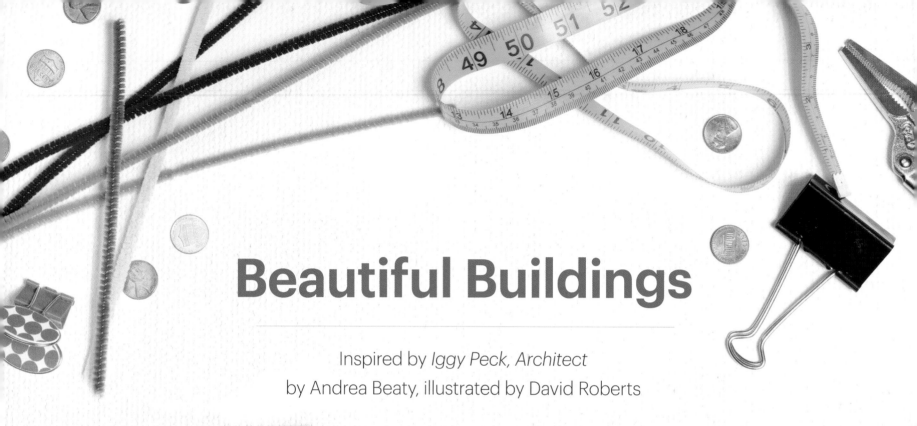

Beautiful Buildings

Inspired by *Iggy Peck, Architect*
by Andrea Beaty, illustrated by David Roberts

Beautiful Buildings

LET'S LOOK AT THE PROBLEM

Iggy Peck began building at the early age of 2, when he built a tower from dirty diapers! As he grows, he continues to build things like a cathedral out of apples and a castle out of chalk. When he gets to second grade, his teacher forbids him to build anything more. But when the class goes on a field trip, it's up to Iggy to rescue them all from trouble.

Why does Iggy's teacher forbid him to build anything in class? What problem arises on the field trip? How does Iggy use his building skills to solve the problem?

MATERIALS

- [ ] Reusable resources such as boxes, cartons, cardboard tubes, craft sticks, toothpicks, paper plates, plastic cups, pipe cleaners, wooden skewers, and drinking straws

- [ ] Connectors such as tape, glue, brads, binder clips, rubber bands, playdough, clay, wire, and cardboard connectors

- [ ] Tools such as scissors, measuring tapes, rolling pins, and pliers

- [ ] Photos or magazine pictures of tall buildings in your community and other locations

- [ ] 100 pennies

- [ ] Paper and markers, crayons, or pencils

TINKER WITH THE MATERIALS

Gather several building materials. What have you built that is really tall? How did you build it? How tall was your building? What if you wanted to build something out of these things (e.g., drinking straws or wooden skewers)? What could you use to hold them together? What do you do to keep your buildings from falling down? (HINT: Try to build "up" with the materials.)

STEM CONCEPTS

balance / design engineering / force / geometry / gravity / measurement / number concepts / patterning / qualities of materials / scientific inquiry / stability

Beautiful Buildings

THE DESIGN CHALLENGE

Making Create a tall building using several different materials.

Engineering Use the materials to create a prototype (model) of a building you see in a photo or picture. Make your model at least two feet tall and sturdy enough to hold the weight of 100 pennies.

WORKING ON THE DESIGN CHALLENGE

- **Think about it.** What kind of building will you make? What will it look like? Draw or sketch your ideas.

  Engineering. Look at the photos or pictures of buildings and choose one to build. What shapes do you see in the building? How are the shapes in the building the same or different? Look at the materials that are available. How will you build a model of the building in the photo? What will you do to make it stable?

- **Build or create it.** Gather your materials and construct your building. Make sure it is strong and sturdy.

  Engineering. How can you combine shapes to make a different shape? Which shapes help make your building strong?

- **Try it.** Does the building stand up on its own?

  Engineering. Does your building look similar to the one in the picture? Measure the height of your building. Is it at least two feet tall? Find out how many pennies it can hold without toppling over.

- **Revise or make it better.** Does it work? If it doesn't, what can you change to make the building better, stronger, or more stable?

  Engineering. Make changes to your structure that will help it hold more pennies. Record how many more pennies the new building can hold.

- **Share.** Tell someone about your building and what it is. Who would use it? What would they use it for?

  Engineering. Draw a picture of your final building and label its parts. Display this picture next to the original sketch of your ideas. Share your drawings with others and talk about how your plans changed once you started building.

Beautiful Buildings

QUESTIONS AND COMMENTS

What other materials could you use to construct a building?

I see you made a pattern in your building with _____ (long/short straws, big/little boxes).

How can you keep your building from falling?

Which part of your building do you think is the strongest? Why do you think so?

BACK TO THE PROBLEM IN THE BOOK

Iggy uses some unusual materials to make his buildings! Do you think someone could actually create those structures and get them to stand up? Why or why not? What materials do you think Iggy might use to make a school? a barn? a baseball stadium? a treehouse?

GOING DEEPER

- Research how buildings are made to survive events like earthquakes, fires, hurricanes, and strong winds. How would you design and build a structure to survive one of these events? What kind of materials would you use?

- Add more details to your buildings by including doors, walls, stories, and a roof. Think about other features you might add, such as arches, fire escapes, balconies, and porches.

- Measure your building. Compare the height of your building with the height of buildings your friends created. Make a graph showing the different heights.

OTHER BOOKS TO USE

Dreaming Up: A Celebration of Building / Christy Hale

First Shapes in Buildings / Penny Ann Lane

How a House Is Built / Gail Gibbons

Box It!

Inspired by *Not a Box*
by Antoinette Portis

Box It!

LET'S LOOK AT THE PROBLEM

Each time someone asks the bunny what he is doing with his box and why, he says, "It's not a box!" Everyone thinks the box is just a box, but the bunny imagines it to be a racecar, a mountain, a building on fire, a robot, a pirate ship, a hot air balloon, a steamboat, or a rocket ship.

Have you ever used a box to make something? If you were the bunny, what would *you* make with just one box?

MATERIALS

- [ ] Reusable resources such as boxes of different sizes and shapes, cardboard, paper plates and cups, and bottle caps
- [ ] Connectors such as glue, brads, wire, tape, cardboard rivets, reusable zip ties, and a low-temperature glue gun
- [ ] Tools such as scissors, child-safe cardboard cutters, wooden skewers, and pliers
- [ ] Items for decorating such as yarn, string, fabric, felt, drinking straws, pom-poms, feathers, googly eyes, stickers, glitter, craft foam, beads, and tissue and construction paper
- [ ] Paper and markers, crayons, or pencils

Safety note: Adult assistance needed in cutting cardboard

TINKER WITH THE MATERIALS

Explore the boxes. How can you combine them or decorate them? How can you use other materials with the boxes?

Tinker and create with different types of cardboard. Which types are easiest to bend, fold, poke holes in, or cut?

With an adult's help, explore tools and materials for making with cardboard. Try child-safe cardboard cutters, scissors, cardboard rivets, and different types of tape.

STEM CONCEPTS

balance / geometry / design engineering / gravity / motion / physical properties of objects / scientific inquiry / simple machines / spatial relationships

Box It!

THE DESIGN CHALLENGE

Making Use cardboard boxes to create something new.

Engineering Use the boxes to create a game that allows players to score points. (See "Other Resources," on the next page.)

WORKING ON THE DESIGN CHALLENGE

- **Think about it.** What will you make with the cardboard boxes? Is it something the bunny made or something completely different? How will you create it? What materials do you need? Draw or sketch your ideas.

  Engineering. Think about the games you like to play. How do they work? How can you use the boxes and other objects to make a new kind of game? How will players score points? How will points be recorded?

- **Build or create it.** Gather your materials and make your box creation. Decorate it if you like.

  Engineering. Create your game using the materials. Include ways for the player to score points.

- **Try it.** Use your not-a-box.

  Engineering. Test your game by playing it with a friend.

- **Revise or make it better.** Does your creation do what you want it to do? If it doesn't, how can you change it?

  Engineering. What works with your game, and what doesn't? What do you want to change?

- **Share.** Ask someone to guess what you created with your boxes. Invite them to play with you using your creation. Write or dictate a short story about what you made.

  Engineering. Invite someone else to join you in playing your game. Show them how it works. Ask them if they have ideas about how to make it better. If other friends have made games from boxes, set up an arcade and invite others to play.

Box It!

QUESTIONS AND COMMENTS

I wonder what you could make with this cardboard box.

I wonder what would happen if _____.

How will you play with this?

What if you wanted your game or your creation to _____ ? How would you do that?

How will you make your game strong enough that it won't break when people try to play it?

BACK TO THE PROBLEM IN THE BOOK

How does the bunny use his imagination? How did you use yours? What are some other ways the bunny could use a single box?

GOING DEEPER

- What could you make by using only boxes that are shaped like cylinders? Try out your ideas.

- Build something that will cover a five-by-six-foot area.

- Research how to make cardboard linkages or cardboard automata to add motion to your creation (described on page 16 of this book).

- How could you use batteries and bulbs to light up your creation?

- Visit a place (library, makerspace) that has a cardboard laser cutter and watch it in action. How does it work?

- Take apart a small box until it is flat. Use it as a template (pattern) to create a new box from construction paper or cardstock.

OTHER RESOURCES

For inspiration on making games with cardboard, visit www.cainesarcade.com.

OTHER BOOKS TO USE

A Box Story / Kenneth Kit Lamug

Clancy and Millie and the Very Fine House / Libby Gleeson, illustrated by Freya Blackwood

What to Do With a Box / Jane Yolen, illustrated by Chris Sheban

Bug City

Inspired by *Roberto: The Insect Architect*
by Nina Laden

Bug City

LET'S LOOK AT THE PROBLEM

Roberto is not like other termites. Instead of eating wood, he wants to build with it, so he heads to the big city to fulfill his dream of becoming an architect. There he meets several new insect friends who desperately need homes.

Roberto finds it hard to become an architect because he hasn't built anything yet to show people that he can do it. How does he solve this? If you built a home for someone, what would it look like?

- -

MATERIALS

- [ ] Reusable resources such as paper towel rolls, boxes of all types (including cardboard food containers), milk and egg cartons, newspapers, yogurt cups, foam trays, toothpicks, and aluminum foil

- [ ] Connectors such as tape, glue, a low-temperature glue gun, brads, wire, cardboard connectors, binder clips, clothespins, twine, staples and staplers

- [ ] Tools such as scissors, hole punchers, pliers, and measuring tapes

- [ ] Building toys such as LEGO bricks, blocks, small building planks (KEVA, KAPLA, or Dr. Drew's Discovery Blocks), and K'NEX

- [ ] Reference and planning resources such as nonfiction insect books and videos, blueprints, and graph paper

- [ ] Small toy insects

- [ ] An 8 oz. weight

- [ ] Paper and markers, crayons, or pencils

TINKER WITH THE MATERIALS

Choose two or three items. What can you make with them? Add another item. How can you use it to change your structure? How can you connect your items so they stay together?

Examine blueprints. Look at the different symbols and how rooms, doors, and windows are represented. Draw your own blueprint of a building. Construct your building with blocks while using your blueprint as a plan.

STEM CONCEPTS

architecture / design engineering / life sciences (biology, entomology, habitats) / measurement / observation / properties of materials / scientific inquiry / stability / structures

Bug City

THE DESIGN CHALLENGE

Making Build a home for an insect.

Engineering Build a home to meet the needs of a specific insect. The building should be at least two feet tall and sturdy enough to hold an object weighing at least eight ounces. There should be an entrance for a small toy insect (or one you create) that is less than two inches high.

WORKING ON THE DESIGN CHALLENGE

- **Think about it.** What does an insect need in a home? Draw or sketch your ideas for what you will build.

    Engineering. Choose an insect. Look at it in books and videos. If possible, observe a real insect closely. How does it move? What does it eat? How much room does it need? What kind of home will you design to meet this insect's needs? Just as Roberto created a blueprint, draw or sketch your plans, including as much detail as possible.

- **Build or create it.** Gather your materials and build a home for your insect.

    Engineering. Remember that your home must be at least two feet tall and able to hold an eight-ounce weight. Don't forget to create an entrance that is less than two inches high.

- **Try it.** Test your home out. Does it stay together? Do you think it is stable enough for an insect to use?

    Engineering. Is your insect able to fit through the entrance? Is the house at least two feet tall? Does it hold an object weighing at least eight ounces?

- **Revise or make it better.** What about your insect home works, and what doesn't? How can you improve it?

    Engineering. Compare your plan and the home you built. How did making a plan help you? Do you need to go back and revise your plan and your home? How?

- **Share.** Show your plans and your insect home to someone else. Ask for their ideas. How would they have created it?

    Engineering. Make a movie of the toy insect using its new home. Describe the type of insect you built the house for and how your home meets its needs.

Bug City

QUESTIONS AND COMMENTS

Why did you choose your insect?

Tell me about the features of your insect home. How did you make them?

What else could you add to the home?

How is this insect's home the same as or different from your home?

BACK TO THE PROBLEM IN THE BOOK

How does Roberto make sure his buildings meet the needs of their occupants?

What might happen if Roberto's family came to visit him in the big city?

GOING DEEPER

- Brainstorm ways to create a home for actual insects in your area. Think about materials that can stay outside. How will your building attract the insects? Plan and then make the home.

- Research homes made by other types of animals, and choose one to create.

- Research how to make a robotic bug ("brush bot") for your insect home using a toothbrush, battery, LED, small vibrating motor, and decorations.

- Make a stop-motion animation of your toy insect using its new home.

OTHER BOOKS TO USE

The Best Book of Bugs / Claire Llewellyn, illustrated by Chris Forsey, Andrea Ricciardi di Gaudesi, and David Wright

A House Is a House for Me / Mary Ann Hoberman, illustrated by Betty Fraser

Insects and Spiders / Bo Rin, illustrated by Do Gam, edited by Joy Cowley

Build a Bridge

Inspired by *The Three Billy Goats Gruff*
by Paul Galdone

Build a Bridge

LET'S LOOK AT THE PROBLEM

Three billy goats want to go up a hillside to eat some grass. But they have to cross a bridge to get there, and under the bridge lives a mean, ugly old troll who wants to eat them.

How do the goats use their brains and their strength to outsmart the troll? What's another way the goats could get to the hillside without crossing the troll's bridge?

MATERIALS

- [ ] Reusable resources such as paper, newspapers, drinking straws, craft sticks, toothpicks, paper clips, cotton swabs, clay, plastic cups, Styrofoam trays, and cardboard boxes, sheets, and tubes

- [ ] Connectors such as glue, tape, wire, and brads

- [ ] Tools such as scissors, rulers, and measuring tapes

- [ ] Photos of different bridge designs

- [ ] A balance scale and three 5 lb. weights to represent the billy goats

- [ ] Paper and markers, crayons, or pencils

TINKER WITH THE MATERIALS

Tinker with making bridges out of different materials, like toothpicks, drinking straws, paper, rolled-up newspaper, or clay. How will you hold the materials together? Which materials seem stronger than others?

STEM CONCEPTS

balance / force / geometry / gravity / measurement / motion / number concepts / patterns / scientific inquiry / stability / structural engineering

Build a Bridge

THE DESIGN CHALLENGE

Making Build a troll-proof bridge that stands on its own so the goats can cross the river.

Engineering Build a troll-proof bridge that spans at least 10 inches and supports at least five pounds.

WORKING ON THE DESIGN CHALLENGE

- **Think about it.** Look at pictures of different bridges. How will you build your bridge? Draw or sketch your ideas.

    Engineering. What shapes do you notice in the bridge pictures? What ideas does this give you for making your bridge? What items will you use to represent your billy goats? What can you add to the bridge to keep the troll from getting on it?

- **Build or create it.** Gather your materials and build the troll-proof bridge.

    Engineering. Make sure your bridge is strong enough to hold at least one billy goat and includes a feature to keep the troll away.

- **Try it.** See if your bridge will stand on its own without falling over.

    Engineering. Can the billy goats safely cross the bridge? Test your bridge by placing one weight at a time on the bridge until it collapses.

- **Revise or make it better.** Does it work? If it doesn't, what can you change to make it stronger or better?

- **Share.** Act out the story of the three billy goats with your bridge. As part of the story, explain to the goats how you built their new bridge and why it is strong.

    Engineering. Write or tell someone about a problem you ran into while building your bridge. How did you solve it? What have you learned while making your bridge?

Build a Bridge

QUESTIONS AND COMMENTS

What do you think will happen if _____?

What shapes make the strongest bridge?

What tools can you use to measure the bridge?

How much weight do you think your bridge will support?

BACK TO THE PROBLEM IN THE BOOK

Why do you think your bridge design is a good idea for the goats?

GOING DEEPER

- Imagine your bridge must be built over a river that is twice as wide as the original one. Change your design or build a new bridge that spans at least 20 inches and will hold at least one billy goat.

- The river is now open to large boats and ships. They need to pass under the bridge. Build a drawbridge to allow the ships to pass. What additional materials do you need?

- Pretend the troll is jealous and wants a new bridge for himself. Keep in mind he's much bigger than the goats! Build a bridge that can hold double the weight of your current bridge.

- Use sturdy cardboard and connectors or wood scraps, hammers, nails, and other similar materials to build a stronger, more permanent bridge for the goats. Compare the two bridges you made. What do you notice?

OTHER BOOKS TO USE

Pop's Bridge / Eve Bunting, illustrated by C.F. Payne

This Bridge Will Not Be Gray / Dave Eggers, illustrated by Tucker Nichols

Twenty-One Elephants and Still Standing / April Jones Prince, illustrated by François Roca

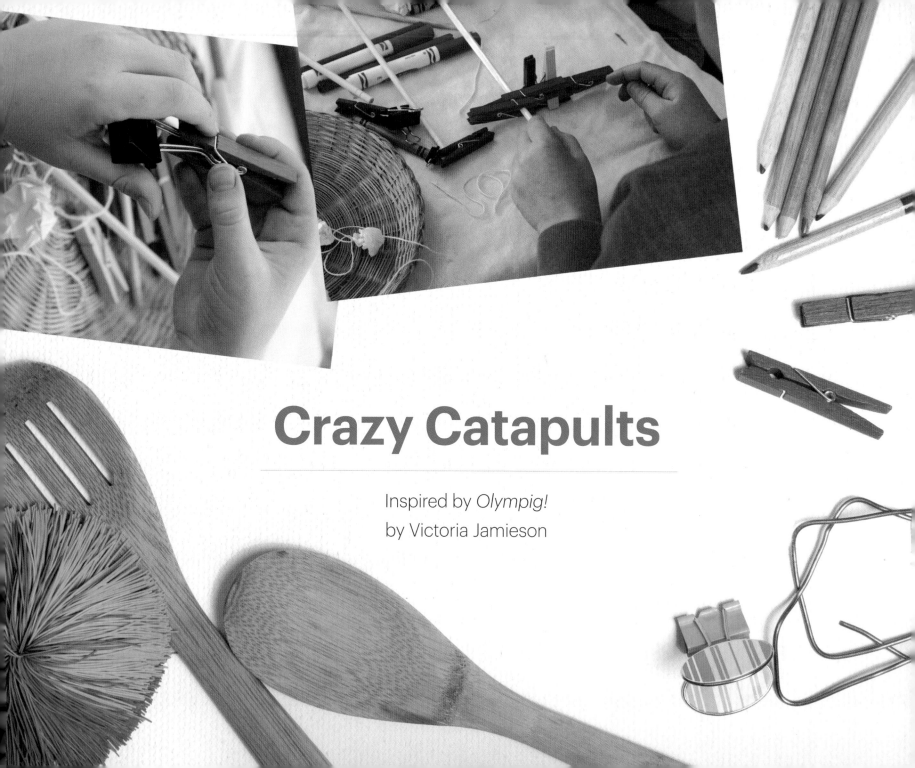

Crazy Catapults

Inspired by *Olympig!*
by Victoria Jamieson

Crazy Catapults

LET'S LOOK AT THE PROBLEM

A pig named Boomer participates in the Animal Olympics. He isn't the fastest or the strongest, but he does work hard. One of the events Boomer has trouble with is the pole vault—he just can't seem to make it over the bar.

Have you ever seen someone pole vaulting? In the pole vault event, athletes use a long pole to propel themselves over a high bar. Catapults also launch objects through the air. The objects being launched are called projectiles. Where have you seen a catapult? A slingshot is one type. Let's explore some ways you can launch objects by building a catapult.

MATERIALS

- ☐ Reusable resources such as craft sticks, tongue depressors, Tinker Toys, wooden or plastic spoons, bottle caps, and wood scraps
- ☐ Connectors such as glue, tape, clothespins, rubber bands, low-temperature glue gun, wire, brads, twine, reusable zip ties, and binder clips
- ☐ Small, lightweight projectiles (objects to be launched) such as pom-poms, crumpled paper balls, cotton balls, table tennis balls, and packing peanuts
- ☐ Photos of catapults
- ☐ Paper and markers, crayons, or pencils

TINKER WITH THE MATERIALS

How can you use and combine some of the materials to launch one of the lightweight objects? (HINT: The trick to a catapult is to launch the projectile from a 45-degree angle. While the concept of 45-degree angles is advanced for this age group, invite children to investigate launching the projectiles by pressing [or pulling] the launching arm all the way, part of the way, most of the way, etc.)

STEM CONCEPTS

design engineering / energy / force / gravity / motion / number concepts / scientific inquiry / simple machines

Crazy Catapults

THE DESIGN CHALLENGE

Making Use a spoon as a catapult to launch a pom-pom or other lightweight object.

Engineering Design and build a catapult that will launch a soft, lightweight object at least five feet.

WORKING ON THE DESIGN CHALLENGE

- **Think about it.** Think and talk about how you will build your catapult. What materials will you need? Draw or sketch your ideas.

   Engineering. What will affect how far the catapult can launch an object? How will you make it sturdy? Which materials are the strongest?

- **Build or create it.** Build your catapult. Predict how far you can send a soft object like a pom-pom or cotton ball.

   Engineering. How will you build your base? Use a lightweight, but strong, material for the throwing arm of your catapult.

- **Try it.** Place a pom-pom or other lightweight object on the end of the throwing arm of the catapult. Launch it! How far does the object go? How accurate is your prediction?

   Engineering. Measure the distance from the catapult to where the object landed. Try pressing down on the arm

of the catapult a little more or a little less. How does this change the distance that the object travels?

- **Revise or make it better.** Does it work? If it doesn't, what can you change?

   Engineering. If you want the object to travel farther, what can you do or change?

- **Share.** Test your catapult against those made by other students. Record how far each object goes.

   Engineering. Show someone how your catapult works. Talk about why your design was more successful or less successful than you expected. What did you learn while building and testing the catapult? Does the other person have ideas for improving it?

Crazy Catapults

QUESTIONS AND COMMENTS

I wonder which would travel farther, heavier or lighter objects.

How can you make your catapult launch the object farther without changing the design? How much farther can the object go?

If you used larger or heavier objects, would the same catapult work? What changes might be necessary?

What happens if you launch more than one pom-pom at once? Do they travel the same distance? Do they go in the same direction?

What if you used something longer than a craft stick, like a ruler or a yardstick? How would your catapult have to change? Would that make the object go farther?

BACK TO THE PROBLEM IN THE BOOK

How is the pole vault different from the catapults you created? How is it similar? If you were to build a catapult to help Boomer over the high bar, how big do you think it would need to be? What materials could you use? (Remember, Boomer weighs a lot!)

OTHER BOOKS TO USE

GOING DEEPER

- Build another catapult using a different design.

- Set up containers (like buckets and plastic bowls and cups) at a distance from your catapult to catch the pom-poms or other soft, lightweight objects. See how accurately you can aim into them. Arrange several containers and assign values to them according to how far away they are from the catapult.

- Design and build a catapult that can move from place to place.

- Research medieval catapults. Use recyclable materials to create models of catapults used in the Middle Ages.

Explore Simple Machines! With 25 Great Projects / Anita Yasuda, illustrated by Bryan Stone

The Knight and the Dragon / Tomie dePaola

Simon and Catapult Man's Perilous Playground Adventure / Norene Smiley, illustrated by Brenda Jones

Float Your Boat

Inspired by *Who Sank the Boat?*
by Pamela Allen

Float Your Boat

LET'S LOOK AT THE PROBLEM

A cow, a donkey, a pig, a sheep, and a mouse take a boat ride. As each one enters, the boat sinks lower and lower, until it finally sinks completely.

The mouse was the smallest animal, but the boat sank after he got in! What do you think happened? What makes an object sink or float?

. . . .

MATERIALS

- ☐ Reusable resources such as aluminum foil
- ☐ Tools such as scissors, measuring tapes, and rulers
- ☐ Objects that sink or float such as pennies, packing peanuts, bottle caps, rubber bands, paper clips, pebbles, different types of balls, and marbles
- ☐ Large container of water
- ☐ Paper and markers, crayons, or pencils

TINKER WITH THE MATERIALS

Which objects do you think will float? Which will sink? Test your predictions. What do you notice? Can you do something with the objects that float so they will sink? Can you find a way to make the objects that sink float instead?

STEM CONCEPTS

buoyancy / density / design engineering / geometry / gravity / measurement / properties of matter / scientific inquiry / sinking and floating

Float Your Boat

THE DESIGN CHALLENGE

Making Use foil to build a boat that floats.

Engineering Use 10-inch square pieces of foil to build boats that float and hold as many pennies (or other lightweight objects) as possible before sinking.

WORKING ON THE DESIGN CHALLENGE

• **Think about it.** How are boats shaped? Look at the materials. How can you form them into a boat that will float? Draw or sketch your ideas.

   Engineering. How can you make a boat that will stay afloat when you add weight to it? Predict the number of pennies your boat will hold.

• **Build or create it.** Build your boat. What shape do you think will work the best?

   Engineering. Build several boats from foil. Make each a different shape.

• **Try it.** Does your boat float? If not, does it sink all at once or over time? Why do you think this happened?

   Engineering. Add pennies one at a time to your boat. How many pennies can you add to your boats before they will sink? Which shape holds the most pennies?

• **Revise or make it better.** If the boat doesn't float, what do you think the reason is? What can you change to make the boat float?

   Engineering. How can you change your boat so that it can carry more weight? Why would making this change work?

• **Share.** Explain to someone how you made your boat, and show them how it works.

   Engineering. Explain to someone which design allows the boat to hold the most weight without sinking and why.

Float Your Boat

QUESTIONS AND COMMENTS

I wonder what would happen if you used wet pennies instead of dry pennies.

What shape do you think will make the best boat for floating? for moving through the water?

What did you think about when you designed your boat?

BACK TO THE PROBLEM IN THE BOOK

The first four animals affect the balance of the boat by where they sit. What happens when the cow gets in on one end? Why? Where does the sheep sit to help keep the boat balanced? How is *your* boat affected by where you place the pennies?

GOING DEEPER

- What other materials could you use to build a boat? How would this affect its ability to hold weight?

- Make a boat that's a different shape than your first one, like a barge or a canoe. Compare how they float and how much weight they can hold. Do you get the same results for both boats? If not, why?

- What would happen if you tried to float your boat in a liquid other than water? Try it to find out.

- How many pennies do you think your boat would hold if it were twice as big? Only half as big?

OTHER BOOKS TO USE

The Gingerbread Boy / Paul Galdone

Mr. Gumpy's Outing / John Burningham

Toy Boat / Randall de Sève, illustrated by Loren Long

Gizmos Galore

Inspired by *Rosie Revere, Engineer* by Andrea Beaty,
illustrated by David Roberts

Gizmos Galore

LET'S LOOK AT THE PROBLEM

Although Rosie is quiet at school, her imagination goes wild at night as she invents all kinds of contraptions. One day her Great-Great-Aunt Rose tells Rosie about all the airplanes she helped build when she was younger. When Great-Great-Aunt Rose tells her about the one goal she didn't achieve—her lifelong dream to fly—Rosie gets to work building a contraption so her aunt can finally fly. But alas, it doesn't fly—it crashes. Was it a failure? Well, you only fail if you quit.

What kinds of materials did Rosie use to build her contraptions? How did she get her ideas? What have you built? Did it work?

MATERIALS

- ☐ Reusable resources such as boxes, cardboard sheets and tubes, craft sticks, fabric scraps, yarn, and corks
- ☐ Connectors such as tape, wire, a low-temperature glue gun, cardboard connectors, and brads
- ☐ Tools such as scissors, child-safe cardboard cutters, measuring tapes, and child-size hammers, screwdrivers, and pliers
- ☐ Everyday objects (some with moving parts) such as a backpack, toothbrush, piggy bank, umbrella, flashlight, or telephone
- ☐ Toys to take apart that have moving parts
- ☐ Objects to put together such as nuts, bolts, clothespins, craft sticks, and wood scraps
- ☐ Paper and markers, crayons, or pencils

Safety note: Adult assistance needed in cutting cardboard

TINKER WITH THE MATERIALS

Take apart objects that have moving parts. Examine the gears, motors, springs, circuitry, or wires on the inside. How are the parts connected? How does the object work? How could you make it work better? Try to reassemble it. If you can't reassemble it, how could you use these parts to create something new?

Explore items like nuts, bolts, clothespins, craft sticks, and wood scraps. Use real tools to put them together to create something new.

STEM CONCEPTS

design engineering / measurement / mechanical engineering / scientific inquiry / simple machines / technology

Gizmos Galore

THE DESIGN CHALLENGE

Making Take an everyday object and find ways to make it better.

Engineering Find a way to improve an everyday object by making it lighter, smaller, more powerful, or able to be used for more than one purpose.

WORKING ON THE DESIGN CHALLENGE

- **Think about it.** Choose an object that you use often. What changes could make it better? How would you make these changes? Draw or sketch your ideas.

   Engineering. What are some ways you could make this object smaller or more compact? How could you make it weigh less? Is there a way to make it more powerful? How could you change it so that it can be used for more than one purpose?

- **Build or create it.** Gather your materials to create your new invention.

- **Try it.** Try your new invention.

   Engineering. How will you determine if it weighs less or is more powerful? How many things can you do with your new invention?

- **Revise or make it better.** Does it work? If it doesn't, what can you change to make it work?

   Engineering. Is there a different material you might use to make your invention even lighter? Could you add another feature to make it more useful?

- **Share.** Tell someone about your invention and how you made it. Ask them if they have ideas about how to make it better.

   Engineering. Create a commercial or advertisement for your new invention that explains how it is better than the original object.

Gizmos Galore

QUESTIONS AND COMMENTS

Why did you choose that object to improve?

Tell me about your invention. What will you name it and why?

What do you think will happen if _____?

What was the most challenging part of making this invention?

BACK TO THE PROBLEM IN THE BOOK

Why do you think Rosie's flying contraption didn't work? How do you think she felt when it didn't fly? Sometimes mistakes allow us to improve our plans. How did Rosie improve her plan?

GOING DEEPER

- What is an engineer? Draw or write your ideas, then share them with others. Interview different types or kinds of engineers to find out what they do.

- Watch the video "Caine's Arcade" (www.cainesarcade.com). Invent a game from cardboard. What simple machines did you use in your invention?

- Take an everyday object like a funnel or a hose and see how many different things you can pretend it is.

- Talk to a person who uses special equipment to assist with movement, such as a wheelchair, walker, crutches, scooter, prosthetic device, page turner, or book holder. Ask the individual what improvements he or she would like for the equipment. Draw or make a model.

OTHER BOOKS TO USE

Papa's Mechanical Fish / Candace Fleming, illustrated by Boris Kulikov

Violet the Pilot / Steve Breen

What Do You Do With an Idea? / Kobi Yamada, illustrated by Mae Besom

Help! It's Stuck!

Inspired by *Stuck*
by Oliver Jeffers

Help! It's Stuck!

LET'S LOOK AT THE PROBLEM

Floyd's kite is stuck in a tree. He tries everything to get it down . . . he throws his shoe, a ladder, a bucket of paint, a car, the letter carrier—even two boats and a whale—at the tree. But they all get stuck. How will Floyd get them all down?

Has something of yours ever gotten stuck? Where? How? How did you get it unstuck?

. . . .

MATERIALS

- [ ] Reusable resources such as sticks, newspapers, chopsticks, wooden spools, playdough, and cardboard tubes
- [ ] Connectors such as brads, tape, glue, clothespins, pipe cleaners, binder clips, Velcro, staples and staplers, twine, and wire
- [ ] Tools such as measuring tapes, "grabber" tools and toys, scissors, pliers, tweezers, tongs, clothespins, and flashlights
- [ ] Soft, lightweight objects for an adult to suspend safely
- [ ] Paper and markers, crayons, or pencils
- [ ] Photos of (or objects with) scissor linkages, such as a scissor lift, extendable makeup mirror, or a scissor grabber

TINKER WITH THE MATERIALS

What kind of motion do you use to grab something? Look at tools that grab things, like tweezers, binder clips, tongs, clothespins, and "grabber" tools and toys. How do they work? Try using these objects to pick things up or reach things. How could you make your own grabber?

Investigate a grabber tool used to pick up items out of reach. How does it work? Take apart an old grabber arm. How would you create your own?

Look at pictures or examples of scissor linkages (such as on page 54). Using 1½-inch-wide cardboard strips or large craft sticks and brads, try to create a scissor linkage. (HINT: Make holes in the strips with a wooden skewer. Take two strips to create an X and connect in the center with a brad. Make several of these. Now connect them together on the ends with brads. Moving the legs of the first cardboard X will create a gadget that will extend to reach something.)

STEM CONCEPTS

design engineering / force / gravity / measurement / observation / problem solving / simple machines

Help! It's Stuck!

WORKING ON THE DESIGN CHALLENGE

- **Think about it.** Talk about your ideas. What object will you try to reach? Where is it? What materials do you have that might work to build your contraption? Draw or sketch your ideas.

    Engineering. How is the object positioned overhead? How far away is it? How will you build something to get it down without using a ladder or furniture to climb on?

- **Build or create it.** Gather your materials and put together your contraption.

    Engineering. How is the object attached (tape, Velcro, magnet, hook) overhead? What type of action will your contraption need to do (lift, pull, push, slide, grab)?

- **Try it.** Test out your contraption. Does it work? Are you able to get the object?

- **Revise or make it better.** If you aren't able to retrieve the object, why not? What can you change to make your creation work better? Try it again.

    Engineering. What works and what doesn't? Are there other materials that might work better?

- **Share.** Tell someone your story about how you retrieved the object. Ask them what they would have tried. Brainstorm new ideas for getting something unstuck.

    Engineering. Make an infomercial for your contraption. Demonstrate how it works. Tell how it could be used to retrieve other objects. Show how your contraption could help people such as senior citizens or people with limited mobility.

Help! It's Stuck!

QUESTIONS AND COMMENTS

Tell me how this works.

I wonder why your contraption keeps falling apart. What could you do to make it more stable?

What did you notice about _____?

What if your attempts to get the object down only make it *more* stuck? What could you do?

How will you decide how long to make your contraption if you can't reach it to measure?

BACK TO THE PROBLEM IN THE BOOK

Do you think your contraption would help Floyd get his kite out of the tree? If not, how could you change it?

What else could Floyd have tried?

GOING DEEPER

- How could you change your design so it requires more than one person to operate it? Build and test it.

- Add moving parts to your machine. What other materials do you need?

- Think about other places where an object might get stuck—down a storm drain, between rocks in a stream, or behind a big, heavy piece of furniture. Choose one of these situations and create something that would retrieve the stuck object.

OTHER BOOKS TO USE

Bubble Gum, Bubble Gum / Lisa Wheeler, illustrated by Laura Huliska-Beith
My Truck Is Stuck! / Kevin Lewis, illustrated by Daniel Kirk
Tikki Tikki Tembo / Arlene Mosel, illustrated by Blair Lent

A House for the
Three Little Pigs

Inspired by *The Three Little Pigs*
by Paul Galdone

A House for the Three Little Pigs

LET'S LOOK AT THE PROBLEM

Each of the three little pigs chooses a different building material—straw, sticks, and bricks—to make a house. But the wolf keeps blowing down their houses.

Why was the wolf able to blow down the straw house and the stick house but not the brick house? What could the first two pigs have done to keep the wolf from blowing their houses down?

. . . .

MATERIALS

- ☐ Reusable resources such as drinking straws, wooden skewers, craft sticks, toothpicks, unsharpened pencils, wood scraps, sticks, coffee stirrers, pine needles, and paper cups

- ☐ Connectors such as tape, binder clips, glue, clay, paper clips, and staples and staplers

- ☐ Tools such as scissors, measuring tapes, and rulers

- ☐ Building toys such as LEGO bricks, blocks, small building planks (KEVA, KAPLA, or Dr. Drew's Discovery Blocks), and K'NEX

- ☐ A device or process to make wind such as a fan or waving a magazine or newspaper

- ☐ Paper and markers, crayons, or pencils

TINKER WITH THE MATERIALS

Explore the materials in an open area. Which materials are stronger than others? How can you use the connectors to attach the materials securely?

STEM CONCEPTS

force / geometry / gravity / measurement / number concepts / properties of matter / scientific inquiry / simple machines / structural engineering

A House for the Three Little Pigs

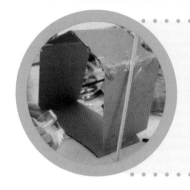

THE DESIGN CHALLENGE

Making Select materials to build a house.

Engineering Using straw-like, stick-like, and brick-like materials, build a strong house that won't fall down when the wind blows at different speeds.

WORKING ON THE DESIGN CHALLENGE

- **Think about it.** Use a fan or another wind-making device to explore the force of wind. Think about why the straw house and the stick house blew down. How will you build your house? What will you do to make it strong and stable? Draw or sketch your ideas.

  Engineering. How will you design your house so the wolf can't get in? How can you outsmart the wolf so he can't blow down your house or get in another way?

- **Build or create it.** Gather your materials to build the house. Make sure that it is strong and sturdy.

  Engineering. How will you build a foundation? a roof? windows? doors?

- **Try it.** Does the house stand up on its own?

  Engineering. Is there a door that opens and closes so the pigs can get in and out? Will your house stand up if the fan is on low, medium, or high? Is there another way for the wolf to get inside your house?

- **Revise or make it better.** If your house doesn't stand up on its own, what can you change to make it better, stronger, or more stable? What material might you try next?

  Engineering. What can you change or add to your house so the pigs are safe and the wolf cannot blow it down or get in another way?

- **Share.** Tell someone about your house and how you made it. Ask them if they have ideas about how to make it better.

  Engineering. Ask another person to test the strength of your house. Can they blow it down if they try? Work with this person to find ways to make your house stronger.

A House for the Three Little Pigs

QUESTIONS AND COMMENTS

What do you think will happen if _____?

I wonder if your house will stay up when wind blows on it. How can we find out?

Does the size or shape of your house affect how sturdy it is? What else affects the sturdiness?

BACK TO THE PROBLEM IN THE BOOK

How does the house you built compare with the houses the pigs build in *The Three Little Pigs*? Do you think the three little pigs would want to or be able to make the house you built? Why or why not?

GOING DEEPER

- Add a new material (such as wood blocks) and a new connector (such as duct tape). How do these additions change what you can make?

- In addition to using a fan, what is another way you can test the strength of the house you built?

- Take a walk in the neighborhood or look at pictures of buildings. What shapes do you see? Try creating some of these shapes in your building. Which shapes are the strongest and support the most weight?

OTHER BOOKS TO USE

The Three Horrid Little Pigs / Liz Pichon
The Three Little Pigs: An Architectural Tale / Steven Guarnaccia
The True Story of the 3 Little Pigs! / Jon Scieszka, illustrated by Lane Smith

If the Shoe Fits

Inspired by *The Elves and the Shoemaker*
by Jim LaMarche

If the Shoe Fits

LET'S LOOK AT THE PROBLEM

One day, the shoemaker has only enough leather for one pair of shoes. He cuts it, and in the middle of the night elves use it to make a pair of shoes. Each night the shoemaker leaves more and more leather on the workbench, and the elves make more and more shoes. The elves leave after the shoemaker and his wife make clothes for them.

What other tools and materials could the elves use to make shoes? What tools and materials would you use to make a pair of shoes?

- -

MATERIALS

☐ Reusable resources such as heavy paper, cardstock, cardboard, string, yarn, fabric, felt, foil, plastic wrap, sponges, bubble wrap, foam, and shoelaces

☐ Connectors such as tape, glue, a low-temperature glue gun, and Velcro fasteners

☐ Tools such as scissors, measuring tapes, rulers, dull darning needles, and mesh plastic canvases

☐ Old shoes to take apart such as light-up sneakers, tap shoes, fluffy slippers, or shoes with roller skates; an old sneaker cut lengthwise so the layers are visible (optional)

☐ Items for decorating the shoes such as buttons, fabric markers, feathers, pom-poms, glitter, and embroidery floss

☐ Paper and markers, crayons, or pencils

TINKER WITH THE MATERIALS

Place the materials on a table. Which materials are good for making shoes? Why? Trace around your shoes (or ask for help to trace around your shoes) on cardboard, cardstock, or heavy paper and cut them out. Decorate your shoes any way you choose.

Take apart old shoes to see how they are made. Save the parts and create a new style by mixing and matching parts and pieces.

Tinker with an old pair of light-up sneakers. How do they work? Where is the battery? How and when do they light up?

Take apart and find out what's inside other old shoes with special features, such as roller skates, squeaky toddler shoes, fluffy slippers, or tap shoes.

STEM CONCEPTS

geometry / life sciences (human body) / measurement / number concepts / patterns / properties of materials / scientific inquiry / structural engineering / symmetry

If the Shoe Fits

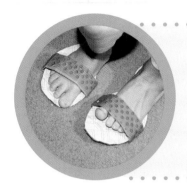

THE DESIGN CHALLENGE

Making   Design and create a pair of shoes for the shoemaker.

Engineering   Pick an activity or a sport. Design and make a pair of shoes to use for that activity or sport (for example, shoes to wear in the rain, shoes to play basketball in, or shoes to jump in).

WORKING ON THE DESIGN CHALLENGE

- **Think about it.** Look around at the different shoes you and your classmates are wearing. What will you need to do first? Draw or sketch your ideas.

    Engineering. Look at different types of shoes (hiking boots, snow or rain boots, sneakers, ballet shoes) to determine how the construction of certain shoes supports their purpose. Decide what kind of shoes you will make and what activity you will use them for.

- **Build or create it.** Gather your materials and make your shoes.

    Engineering. What materials will you use to help make the shoes comfortable? flexible? What material will you use to help prevent slipping?

- **Try it.** Try them on. Do they fit? Do they stay on your feet when you walk? What happens if you run or jump in them?

    Engineering. Do the shoes you made help you perform better?

- **Revise or make it better.** If the shoes don't work, what can you change to make them better?

- **Share.** Tell someone else about how you made your shoes. Ask them for their ideas about what they would do differently or how they would improve them.

    Engineering. Compare the shoes you created with manufactured shoes. What do you notice?

If the Shoe Fits

QUESTIONS AND COMMENTS

I wonder what would happen if you _____.

Tell me what you are doing.

How would you change the shoes so they fit someone with big feet?

What kind of shoes would you make for someone who likes to go outside in cold weather?

Tell me how you made your shoes stay on your feet.

Why do some shoes have smoother soles than others?

BACK TO THE PROBLEM IN THE BOOK

Are you using the same tools to make your shoes as the ones the elves use in the story? What do you think the elves would say about the shoes you created?

GOING DEEPER

- Look at the difference between a shoe for a left foot and one for a right foot. What is the same; what is different? How do you need to modify your design so you can make a pair of shoes (one for the left foot and one for the right)?

- Make a pair of shoes with shoelaces. Did it work out? Why or why not?

- Make shoes using different materials, such as paper, fabric, vinyl, cardboard, plastic, or leather. What tools would you use for the different materials?

- How could you add lights to your shoes?

- Using a foot measurer or ruler, design and create a custom pair of shoes for your teacher or a friend. Interview them to find their favorite color, fabric, and style. Sketch the shoes and get input from your "customer" before making them.

- Watch a video of athletes playing their sport. Pay careful attention to how their feet move. Do they jump, kick, slide, grip, or run? How would your shoe design change based on these actions?

OTHER BOOKS TO USE

Pete the Cat: I Love My White Shoes / Eric Litwin, illustrated by James Dean

Shoes for Me! / Sue Fliess, illustrated by Mike Laughead

Shoes, Shoes, Shoes / Ann Morris

Juice It!

Inspired by *Caterina and the Lemonade Stand*
by Erin Eitter Kono

Juice It!

LET'S LOOK AT THE PROBLEM

Caterina decides to build a lemonade stand to earn enough money to buy herself a scooter. She quickly learns that a lot of her friends have lemonade stands as well. How can she make what she sells in her stand unique?

There are often many ways to make your creation stand out from others'. What other solutions could Caterina have tried? What might have happened if she hadn't tried to make her lemonade different from the others'?

What are your favorite juices? Have you ever tried inventing your own? What kind do you think you would make?

MATERIALS

- [ ] Reusable resources such as tongue depressors, drinking straws, plastic bottles and cups, clay, and playdough
- [ ] Kitchen tools such as gadgets for juicing, knives for cutting fruit, unbreakable bowls and pitchers, strainers, and measuring spoons
- [ ] Fruits for juicing and sweetener
- [ ] Sealable plastic sandwich bags
- [ ] Paper and markers, crayons, or pencils

TINKER WITH THE MATERIALS

Taste some of the fruits before you juice them. Then use the juicing tools to squeeze juice from the fruits to make a drink. How is the juice drink similar to and different from the fruit slices?

Try adding a small amount of sweetener to your juice. How does it taste?

Try making juice using cut fruit, a plastic sandwich bag, and a drinking straw. How would you do it?

Tinker with kitchen gadgets using clay or playdough.

STEM CONCEPTS

chemistry / design engineering / graphing / health and nutrition / measurement / nature / physical science / plants / quantity / scientific inquiry / simple machines

Juice It!

THE DESIGN CHALLENGE

Making Create a fruit-flavored drink that is unique, tasty, and has a catchy name.

Engineering Invent a new tool for juicing and name it.

WORKING ON THE DESIGN CHALLENGE

- **Think about it.** What flavor of fruit drink do you want to make? What will you call your drink? How will you get the juice out of the fruit? Explore the tools you have available and how they work. Draw or sketch your idea.

    Engineering. Think about a new tool you could make to extract the juice from a fruit. How will it work? Why is that the best design? What will you call it?

- **Build or create it.** Choose one or more types of fruit. Use juicing tools to squeeze and strain the juice. Add sweetener if you like.

    Engineering. Use the materials to create a new tool for making fruit juice. Then use it to create unique, tasty fruit-flavored drinks and give each a name. Give your juicing tool a catchy name, too. Record your recipes.

- **Try it.** Taste the juice you made.

    Engineering. Describe the taste. Is it sour? sweet? tangy?

- **Revise or make it better.** Do you like your juice? If you don't like it, how can you change it to make it better? What additional ingredients do you think would make it taste good? Does the color make you want to drink it, or is the color unappetizing? What could you do to make it look more appealing?

    Engineering. How well does your juicer work? What could you change so you can extract more juice from the fruit to make a larger quantity of drinks?

- **Share.** Tell someone about your drink. Ask them to taste the drink and tell you whether they liked it. Tally or record their votes. Have them try to guess what fruit(s) you used.

    Engineering. Make a commercial to demonstrate your juicing tool and explain how it works. Survey your customers to find the most popular flavors, and graph the results.

Juice It!

QUESTIONS AND COMMENTS

How could you get juice from a fruit without a juicer?

What would you do to make juice for five people? ten?

Tell me how you made your juice.

BACK TO THE PROBLEM IN THE BOOK

How does Caterina come up with the idea that made her lemonade unique? Who helps her? How did *you* work with other people to come up with your idea?

GOING DEEPER

- Besides fruit, what other ingredients could you add to your drink? Think about how to balance different tastes, like sweet, sour, bitter, and salty. Try out some of your ideas.

- Work in a small group to perfect a juicer that will make a large quantity of juice at one time (or make several smaller juicers). Then create a company name, a logo, and signs, and advertise and sell your drink to other students in your class or other classes.

- Investigate a commercial juicer. How does it work? What are the important parts? Use what you learn to design and build your own motorized juicer.

OTHER BOOKS TO USE

Lemonade for Sale / Stuart J. Murphy, illustrated by Tricia Tusa

Lemonade in Winter: A Book About Two Kids Counting Money / Emily Jenkins, illustrated by G. Brian Karas

Once Upon a Company...: A True Story / Wendy Anderson Halperin

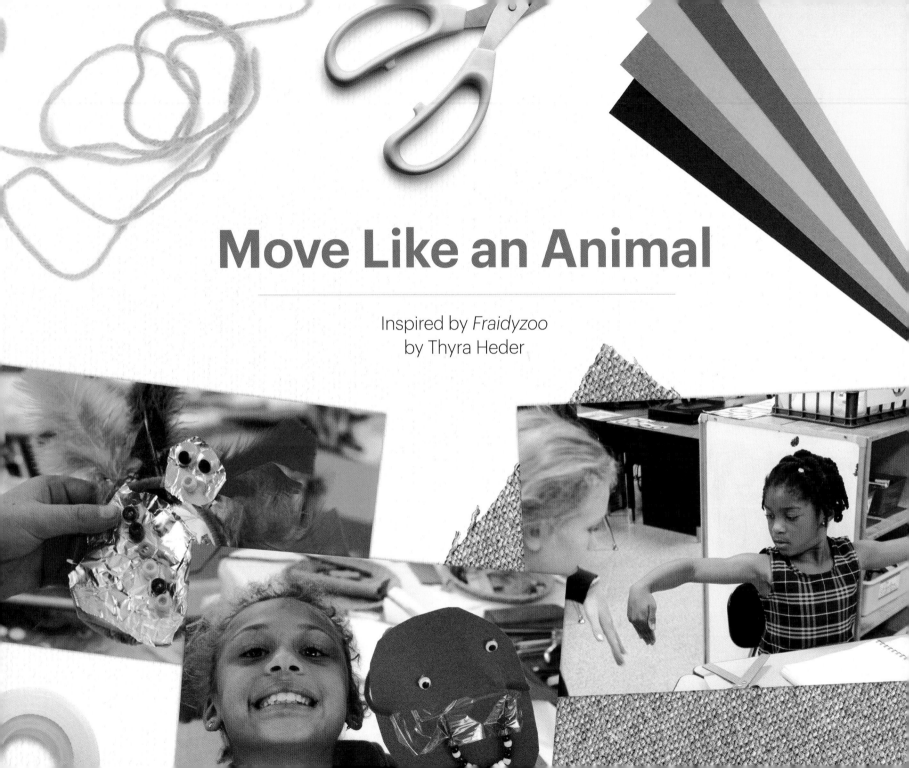

Move Like an Animal

Inspired by *Fraidyzoo*
by Thyra Heder

Move Like an Animal

LET'S LOOK AT THE PROBLEM

Little T's family wants to go to the zoo, but Little T is afraid. She can't remember what she's afraid of, so to help her remember, her family designs and creates costumes and imitates animal movements.

Have you ever been afraid of going someplace the same way that Little T is afraid of going to the zoo? What did your family do to help you feel less scared about going?

• •

MATERIALS

- [ ] Reusable resources such as cardboard, cardstock, construction paper, foam, fabric, craft sticks, and wooden skewers or chopsticks

- [ ] Connectors such as tape, brads, cardboard rivets, glue, staples and staplers, and Velcro

- [ ] Tools such as scissors, child-safe cardboard cutters, paintbrushes, measuring tapes, rulers, dull darning needles, and mesh plastic canvases

- [ ] Items for decorating the masks or costumes such as paints, fabric markers, thread, googly eyes, yarn, felt, pipe cleaners, buttons, embroidery floss, and pom-poms

- [ ] Picture books, photos, or videos of animals

- [ ] Paper and markers, crayons, or pencils

Safety note: Adult assistance needed in cutting cardboard

TINKER WITH THE MATERIALS

Look at and feel the materials. Which animals do you think about while you are exploring the materials? Which materials have textures like the skin of different animals?

Use cardboard and a child-safe cardboard cutter to cut out shapes (or use precut cardboard pieces). Place the cardboard on a piece of foam and poke holes in the cardboard with a wooden skewer. Attach the cardboard shapes with brads or cardboard rivets and explore how to move them.

STEM CONCEPTS

design engineering / geometry / life sciences (animal motions) / measurement / mechanical linkages / number concepts / observation / patterns / technology / tool use

Move Like an Animal

THE DESIGN CHALLENGE

Making Create a zoo animal mask or costume.

Engineering Create your own animal costume that looks like that animal and lets you move like it.

WORKING ON THE DESIGN CHALLENGE

- **Think about it.** Select an animal. Look at photos and videos of it. Carefully notice its features and watch how it moves. Draw or sketch your plan for a mask or costume. How will you make sure it fits you?

    Engineering. Choose an animal and look closely at the different parts of that animal's body. Does it have pincers that open? A tail that wags? How does it move? How will the costume allow you to move the way the animal moves?

- **Build or create it.** Gather your materials and create the mask or costume. Refer to the pictures and your plan.

    Engineering. How will you create the moving parts?

- **Try it.** Compare your costume to the photo or video.

    Engineering. Does your costume fit your body? What feature does your costume include so you can move like the animal?

- **Revise or make it better.** If your mask or costume does not look like the animal, how will you change it so it does?

    Engineering. If your costume doesn't fit or move the way you wanted it to, what changes can you make to improve it or make it better?

- **Share.** Put your mask or costume on and show it to someone else. See if they can guess what animal you are. If they can't, move around the room the way that animal would move and make noises like that animal. Can they guess the animal now?

    Engineering. Show someone else the features of your costume that you included to imitate the animal's movement. Ask them for their ideas on how to improve on your design.

Move Like an Animal

QUESTIONS AND COMMENTS

Tell me about your costume.

How does your animal move? What body part(s) does it need to move that way?

How is your animal mask or costume the same as someone else's? How is it different?

BACK TO THE PROBLEM IN THE BOOK

Does your mask or costume look like one in *Fraidyzoo*? Do you think your mask or costume would help someone like Little T who is afraid of zoo animals?

GOING DEEPER

- How could you make an animal costume that is twice as large as the one you created?

- Create an adult and baby costume of the same animal.

- Create an animal's skeleton using cardboard strips and brads. Add features with markers and decorative materials.

- Can you make the eyes of your animal light up? Can you record a sound for your animal?

- Make a movie or stop-motion animation with a story about your animal.

OTHER BOOKS TO USE

Put Me in the Zoo / Robert Lopshire

A Sick Day for Amos McGee / Philip C. Stead, illustrated by Erin E. Stead

What If You Had...!? (series) / Sandra Markle, illustrated by Howard McWilliam

Paper Airplanes

Inspired by *The Great Paper Caper*
by Oliver Jeffers

Paper Airplanes

LET'S LOOK AT THE PROBLEM

The forest animals' homes are disappearing. All of the trees are being cut down! The animals meet up to try to figure out the mystery. They discover that the bear has been stealing the branches to create not-very-good paper airplanes for a contest.

Have you ever made a paper airplane? How well did it fly?

MATERIALS

- ☐ Reusable resources such as copy and printer paper, newspaper, and magazine pages
- ☐ Small weights such as paper clips and brads
- ☐ Paper and markers, crayons, or pencils
- ☐ Connectors such as tape and staples and staplers (optional)

TINKER WITH THE MATERIALS

As you feel and fold the different papers, think about which one(s) you want to use to make a paper airplane.

Take apart or unfold some paper airplanes to figure out how they were made. Try to fold them back again.

Play with paper airplanes that have already been made.

STEM CONCEPTS

aerodynamics / drag / force / geometry / lift / measurement / motion / scientific inquiry / structural engineering / thrust / wind

Paper Airplanes

WORKING ON THE DESIGN CHALLENGE

- **Think about it.** Look at paper airplanes in a book or online. What do you learn about making them? What type of paper will you use? What shape will you make your airplane? Draw or sketch your ideas.

    Engineering. Look at complex paper airplane designs in a book or online. Will you choose one of these to make or design your own? Which paper will work best with the design? How will you create it so that it flies even when you add a weight to it?

- **Build or create it.** Fold the paper into an airplane.

- **Try it.** Test out your airplane. Does it fly?

    Engineering. How far does your plane go? Does it fly the same distance each time? Create a chart that shows the distance your plane flies each time.

- **Revise or make it better.** If it doesn't work, what can you change to make it better?

    Engineering. What happens if you add a weight to the plane? Does it make a difference where you attach the weight or how heavy the weight is? Make another chart that shows the distance your plane flies each time. What happens if you use another type of paper? Test it with a weight and make another chart.

- **Share.** Tell someone about your airplane. Ask them how they might make one.

    Engineering. Show someone your charts and explain what the charts show about how your planes fly.

Paper Airplanes

QUESTIONS AND COMMENTS

Tell me about your airplane.

How does your airplane fly when you change ____?

I wonder how____.

What can you do to make your airplane fly farther? higher? slower? faster?

BACK TO THE PROBLEM IN THE BOOK

Is the airplane you made good enough to win a paper airplane contest? If not, how could you improve it so it might win a contest?

GOING DEEPER

- How would you make a plane that is half the size of the plane you have made? Would it fly better?

- Does your plane fly better outside or inside?

- Create a plane that flies well in the wind.

- Make two paper airplanes: one with a large wing area and one with a sleeker design. With a friend, launch the two airplanes at the same time. Compare them. Which flew the fastest? Which flew the farthest? Why?

OTHER BOOKS TO USE

Float / Daniel Miyares

Kids' Paper Airplane Book / Ken Blackburn and Jeff Lammers

Whoosh! Easy Paper Airplanes for Kids: Color, Fold, and Fly! / Amy Naylor, illustrated by Kimberly Schwede

Pet Carrier

Inspired by *A Home for Dixie: The True Story of a Rescued Puppy*
by Emma Jackson, photographs by Bob Carey

Pet Carrier

LET'S LOOK AT THE PROBLEM

More than anything else, Emma wants her own puppy. After asking and asking her parents, they finally agree. They decide to rescue a puppy from an animal shelter.

How do they get the puppy from the animal shelter to their home? What do you think is the best way to carry the puppy and take care of its needs?

MATERIALS

- [ ] Reusable resources such as boxes, cardboard, pipe cleaners, string, fabric, and newspaper

- [ ] Connectors such as tape, brads, glue, wire, and staples and staplers

- [ ] Tools such as scissors, measuring tapes, child-safe cardboard cutters, and rulers

- [ ] A balance scale and a 5 lb. weight

- [ ] Pet care items such as unbreakable water bowls, pet toys, and blankets

- [ ] Paper and markers, crayons, or pencils

Safety note: Adult assistance needed in cutting cardboard

TINKER WITH THE MATERIALS

Think about how the materials might fit together to make a sturdy pet carrier. Experiment with different ways to use the connectors, tools, and reusable resources.

STEM CONCEPTS

design engineering / geometry / gravity / life sciences / measurement / scientific inquiry / simple machines

Pet Carrier

THE DESIGN CHALLENGE

Making Design and construct a carrier that pet owners can use to carry animals to and from a shelter.

Engineering Design a pet carrier that is strong enough to carry a five-pound pet and other pet care items.

WORKING ON THE DESIGN CHALLENGE

- **Think about it.** What animal will you be carrying? What kind of space does it need? How will you make sure the carrier is secure when your pet is inside it? Draw or sketch your ideas.

    Engineering. How do you care for your pet? How will you make your carrier strong enough to hold your pet? How will you hold the pet carrier?

- **Build or create it.** Gather the materials you need and build your carrier.

    Engineering. Think about how you will keep your pet safe in the carrier.

- **Try it.** Is your pet carrier secure and sturdy enough to carry an animal?

    Engineering. Does your pet carrier have a door that opens and closes? Pick up your pet carrier by the

handle. What happens when you put a five-pound weight into the carrier? What features and items did you include to care for your pet while it is in the carrier?

- **Revise or make it better.** Does it work? If it doesn't, what can you change to make it better?

    Engineering. How can you change the handle and the overall construction of the carrier to hold a pet and the materials it needs to have inside the carrier?

- **Share.** Tell someone about your pet carrier. Show them how it works. Ask them if they have ideas about how to improve it.

    Engineering. Explain to someone the features of your pet carrier, including the pet care materials inside of it, why they are necessary, and how you designed the carrier to accommodate those materials.

Pet Carrier

QUESTIONS AND COMMENTS

What do you think will happen if _____?

Tell me about your pet.

Tell me about your pet carrier.

How could you change your design so that it _____?

BACK TO THE PROBLEM IN THE BOOK

Do you think your pet carrier is sturdy enough for Emma to use to bring her puppy home? Why or why not?

What kind of carrier would Emma need if she adopted a goldfish?

GOING DEEPER

- How would you design a pet carrier for a pet ant? How about for a pet snake?

- How would you design a pet carrier for a pet that weighed 10 pounds?

- How would you design your pet carrier so that a nervous or frightened pet would feel safe?

OTHER BOOKS TO USE

Before You Were Mine / Maribeth Boelts, illustrated by David Walker

A Home for Dakota / Jan Zita Grover, illustrated by Nancy Lane

Yoda: The Story of a Cat and His Kittens / Beth Stern, illustrated by Devin Crane

Repurpose It!

Inspired by *The Most Magnificent Thing*
by Ashley Spires

Repurpose It!

LET'S LOOK AT THE PROBLEM

A young girl decides she wants to make something magnificent. She has an idea of what it should look like and what it would do, but she gets frustrated after trying to make it and failing over and over again. The dog that is her best friend convinces her she needs a break. After a walk, her mind is clear and she is finally able to create her magnificent something.

Have you ever been frustrated when you are unable to make or do what you planned? What did you do?

MATERIALS

- [ ] Reusable resources such as boxes, string, old CDs and cases, PVC pipes, ice trays, paper plates, plastic cups, wooden skewers, unbreakable mirrors, corks, wooden spools, funnels, clay, balls and marbles, and parts from broken toys

- [ ] Connectors such as glue, brads, tape, clothespins, wire, magnets, and Velcro

- [ ] Tools such as child-size hammers and screwdrivers, safety goggles, pulleys, scissors, pliers, staples and staplers, and a low-temperature glue gun

- [ ] Old toys to take apart such as a cash register, toy car, battery-operated plush toy, or toy robot

- [ ] Paper and markers, crayons, or pencils

TINKER WITH THE MATERIALS

Take apart an old toy such as a cash register, a toy car, a battery-operated plush toy, a windup toy, or a toy robot. How is the toy put together? Think about some of the things you can do with the parts and pieces of the toy to create something new.

STEM CONCEPTS

design engineering / number concepts / physical properties of objects / scientific inquiry

Repurpose It!

THE DESIGN CHALLENGE

Making Create anything using four objects.

Engineering Use four objects to create something useful to help solve a problem or make a task easier. (HINT: You might make something to keep shoelaces from untying or to help someone carry a heavy backpack, clean up a spill, or feed the class pet.)

WORKING ON THE DESIGN CHALLENGE

- **Think about it.** Look at all the materials and think about all the different ways they might be used. Select four objects that can be used together to create something new. Draw or sketch your idea. What will you name it?

  Engineering. What problem will your creation solve, or how will it help make a task easier?

- **Build or create it.** Make sure you use all four objects in your creation. How will you put them together?

- **Try it.** Are you satisfied with your creation? Why or why not?

  Engineering. Test out your invention. What problem are you trying to solve? Describe what works and what does not.

- **Revise or make it better.** What would you like to change about your invention? Why?

  Engineering. Does it solve the problem or make a task easier? If not, how can you change it to make it better?

- **Share.** Write or dictate a story about your invention and how you built it.

  Engineering. Show someone how your invention works and who might use it. Ask them to try it and suggest any ideas about how to improve it. Are they able to make it solve the problem?

Repurpose It!

QUESTIONS AND COMMENTS

I wonder what would happen if _____.

Tell me about your invention.

What other ways could you use these things?

BACK TO THE PROBLEM IN THE BOOK

Would you describe your creation as "magnificent"? Why or why not?

GOING DEEPER

- Create step-by-step directions that show how you made your creation.

- When you add more materials, such as small hobby motors or buzzers, how does that change what you created?

- Create a contraption that uses all the different types of simple machines (wheels and axles, levers, inclined planes, wedges, pulleys, and screws).

OTHER BOOKS TO USE

Awesome Dawson / Chris Gall

The Branch / Mireille Messier, illustrated by Pierre Pratt

Choose to Reuse / Lisa Bullard, illustrated by Wes Thomas

Roller Coaster

Inspired by *Roller Coaster*
by Marla Frazee

Roller Coaster

LET'S LOOK AT THE PROBLEM

A long line of people appears at a fairground ready to ride a roller coaster named Rocket. As people get closer to the front of the line, many change their mind about getting on the roller coaster. Some of them are excited and scared; others appear calm and collected. The roller coaster twists, turns, and loops.

Have you ever been on a roller coaster? How can you create something that maneuvers and moves the same way a roller coaster does?

. . . .

MATERIALS

- [ ] Reusable resources such as PVC pipes and pool noodles, foam insulation tubes, and cardboard tubes (cut in half lengthwise)
- [ ] Connectors such as tape, pipe cleaners, glue, and wire
- [ ] Objects to roll such as small balls or marbles
- [ ] A stopwatch
- [ ] Paper and markers, crayons, or pencils

TINKER WITH THE MATERIALS

Look at all of the materials and find the ones that roll. Explore how well they roll on or inside some of the other items.

Investigate rolling balls down ramps. Which balls roll faster? How can you change the ramp to make them roll faster?

STEM CONCEPTS

centrifugal force / force / gravity / measurement / motion / scientific inquiry / simple machines (inclined planes) / speed / structural engineering / velocity

Roller Coaster

THE DESIGN CHALLENGE

Making Design a marble run by setting up cardboard tubes in different ways to make the marbles roll at different speeds.

Engineering Using pool noodles, marbles, and other materials, set up a roller coaster that includes a series of tricks, like turns, loops, and twists.

WORKING ON THE DESIGN CHALLENGE

- **Think about it.** How will you set up your marble run? What materials will you use? How tall will it be? How long or how wide will it be? How will you try it in different locations? Draw or sketch your ideas.

    Engineering. If you've been on a roller coaster before, think about what it was like. How will you make your marble roller coaster? How high does it need to be for marbles to make it all the way to the end? How will you keep the marbles from falling off? How long can you make the roller coaster and have the marble reach the end without falling off the track?

- **Build or create it.** Gather your materials and construct your marble run or roller coaster.

    Engineering. Add twists, turns, and loops to your design.

- **Try it.** Test your marble run by placing a marble in the track. How fast does the marble go?

    Engineering. Test your roller coaster by placing a marble in the track. Does the marble stay on the track until the end?

- **Revise or make it better.** If your marble run doesn't work, what can you change to fix it or make it better?

    Engineering. If the marble does not stay on your roller coaster, what can you change to fix it or make it better? If the marble does not make it all the way through a loop or twist on your roller coaster, how can you change the track to get the marble to stay on it?

- **Share.** Test your marble run against the ones your classmates made. Which one is fastest? What do you think made it the fastest?

    Engineering. Share your roller coaster with someone else. When they try your roller coaster, does it work? If not, ask that person to help you find a solution.

Roller Coaster

QUESTIONS AND COMMENTS

What would happen if you _____?

What other tricks could you make your roller coaster do?

What do you notice makes the marbles go faster or slower? How can you make them move even faster?

BACK TO THE PROBLEM IN THE BOOK

Does your marble run or roller coaster go fast like the roller coaster in the story?

GOING DEEPER

- How can you design a smaller roller coaster? Do the marbles go faster or slower than they did in the larger roller coaster?

- How can you design a marble run or roller coaster that uses a large marble?

- Build a marble run or roller coaster that fits in a box that is 36" x 12" x 24" or other specified size.

OTHER BOOKS TO USE

Curious George Roller Coaster / H.A. Rey and Monica Perez

Harriet and the Roller Coaster / Nancy Carlson

The Roller Coaster Kid / Mary Ann Rodman, illustrated by Roger Roth

Squirrel-Proof Birdfeeder

Inspired by *Those Darn Squirrels!*
by Adam Rubin, illustrated by Daniel Salmieri

Squirrel-Proof Birdfeeder

LET'S LOOK AT THE PROBLEM

Old Man Fookwire loves watching and painting pictures of birds. He builds some birdfeeders and fills them with seeds and berries to keep the birds around in the winter—but those darn squirrels keep getting into the birdfeeders and eating all the treats!

What does Old Man Fookwire do to keep the squirrels away? Does it work?

- -

MATERIALS

- ☐ Reusable resources such as boxes, craft sticks, chopsticks, cardboard tubes, plastic spoons, PVC pipes, and plastic cups

- ☐ Connectors such as tape, glue, a low-temperature glue gun, brads, pipe cleaners, twine, wire, and clothespins

- ☐ Tools such as safety goggles; scissors; measuring tapes; paintbrushes; and child-size hammers, screwdrivers, and pliers

- ☐ Items for decorating such as paint, feathers, pom-poms, and stickers

- ☐ Paper and markers, crayons, or pencils

TINKER WITH THE MATERIALS

As you explore the materials, think about which ones might be useful for making something tall.

STEM CONCEPTS

balance / gravity / machines / measurement / number concepts / scientific inquiry / simple machines / stability / structural engineering

Squirrel-Proof Birdfeeder

THE DESIGN CHALLENGE

Making Build a birdfeeder any way you choose.

Engineering Build a stable, freestanding birdfeeder that is as tall as possible.

WORKING ON THE DESIGN CHALLENGE

- **Think about it.** How will you build the birdfeeder? Where will you put the treats? How will birds get to the treats? Draw or sketch your ideas.

  Engineering. How will you build a tall birdfeeder? How can you make sure it is tall enough so squirrels can't get to it? How will you make sure it is stable and won't fall down? Which materials will you use?

- **Build or create it.** Gather your materials and build a birdfeeder.

  Engineering. Figure out how you will make it freestanding.

- **Try it.** Can birds get in and out of your birdfeeder? Is there a place to put birdseed?

  Engineering. Does the birdfeeder stand on its own without toppling over?

- **Revise or make it better.** Does the birdfeeder work? If not, what can you change?

  Engineering. Does it work? If not, what can you change to make it better or more stable so birds can get the seeds and squirrels can't?

- **Share.** Tell someone about your birdfeeder. Show them how it works. Ask them if they have ideas about how to make it better.

  Engineering. Fill your birdfeeder with seed and put it outside. Each day, watch what happens and record it on paper. Use this information to tell a story about your birdfeeder.

Squirrel-Proof Birdfeeder

QUESTIONS AND COMMENTS

What do you think will happen if _____?

Tell me about your birdfeeder.

I wonder how tall your birdfeeder is. How can we find out?

If you were a squirrel, what would you do to get into the birdfeeder?

BACK TO THE PROBLEM IN THE BOOK

Is your birdfeeder squirrel proof? How could you test it to find out?

GOING DEEPER

- In addition to birdseed, what else do birds like to eat? How would you build a birdfeeder to hold that food?

- Pretend you are one of the squirrels trying to get to the birdfeeders. What contraptions would you invent to reach the birdfeeder?

- What kind of birdhouse might different birds live in? Design one for a specific bird.

OTHER BOOKS TO USE

Nuts to You! / Lois Ehlert

The Secret Life of Squirrels / Nancy Rose

The Tale of Squirrel Nutkin / Beatrix Potter

Strike Up the Band

Inspired by *Olivia Forms a Band*
by Ian Falconer

Strike Up the Band

LET'S LOOK AT THE PROBLEM

When Olivia finds out that there isn't going to be a band at the fireworks show, she decides to make her own music. Using pots, pans, her brother's toys, and even her father's suspenders, Olivia forms a band all by herself!

Have you ever seen a one-person band? What do you think about how Olivia constructs her one-person band?

MATERIALS

- [ ] Reusable resources such as paper plates, plastic cups, cardboard boxes, pie pans, cans, plastic eggs, chopsticks, ribbon, playdough, string, and rubber bands
- [ ] Connectors such as tape, glue, a low-temperature glue gun, wire, pipe cleaners, and brads
- [ ] Tools such as measuring tapes, scissors, and paintbrushes
- [ ] Items for decorating such as paint, feathers, pom-poms, glitter, beads, and stickers
- [ ] Musical instruments to display
- [ ] Paper and markers, crayons, or pencils

TINKER WITH THE MATERIALS

Tap, clang, pluck, and combine the materials to discover the different sounds they can produce.

Investigate musical instruments up close. How do they work? What are the different ways you can make sounds (by shaking, hitting, blowing, strumming, tapping). How can you make sounds high/low, loud/soft, fast/slow? Ask a visiting musician to show you how her musical instrument works.

STEM CONCEPTS

air / force / measurement / number concepts / patterns / properties of matter / scientific inquiry / sound / structural engineering / vibration / wind

Strike Up the Band

THE DESIGN CHALLENGE

Making Design and make instruments and noisemakers.

Engineering Create an instrument that has two or more ways to make a sound that can be heard from a distance of at least 30 feet.

WORKING ON THE DESIGN CHALLENGE

- **Think about it.** Examine the instruments and think about how sound is made. Look at the different shapes and sizes of the instruments. Explore the materials. What do you think you can use to make an instrument? How will you produce sound? Draw or sketch your ideas.

    Engineering. How will you design an instrument that makes at least two specific noises that can be heard 30 feet away?

- **Build or create it.** Construct your instrument.

- **Try it.** Does it work? How can you make the sound louder?

    Engineering. Can your instrument be heard 30 feet away? How can you make the sound louder?

- **Revise or make it better.** If it doesn't work, what can you change so it does work?

    Engineering. What can you change so your instrument works better?

- **Share.** Show someone your instrument. Invite them to play it. Ask them how they would improve it.

    Engineering. Ask someone to stand 30 feet away. Play your instrument, and ask the person to describe the sound they hear. Can they guess how the sound is made?

Strike Up the Band

QUESTIONS AND COMMENTS

What do you think will happen if you _____?

I wonder what makes the sounds loud.

How can you make sounds with different parts of your body?

BACK TO THE PROBLEM IN THE BOOK

How does your musical instrument compare to the one Olivia creates?

GOING DEEPER

- Create an instrument that has a high pitch and another that has a low pitch.

- Use a camera to take photos of each step of making your instrument. Use them to make a book about your instrument.

- Make a band with some of your classmates and their instruments. How can you make the instruments sound good together?

- Explore digital music tools like Makey Makey (www.makeymakey.com) to turn everyday objects (like a banana) into a musical instrument.

OTHER BOOKS TO USE

Ah, Music! / Aliki

Max Found Two Sticks / Brian Pinkney

Tito Puente: Mambo King/Rey del Mambo / Monica Brown, illustrated by Rafael López

A Sturdy Nest

Inspired by *Mama Built a Little Nest*
by Jennifer Ward, illustrated by Steve Jenkins

A Sturdy Nest

LET'S LOOK AT THE PROBLEM

Bird nests come in all shapes and sizes. They can be in trees, near water, on beaches, and in the snow. Birds use what is around them to build their nests, so they can be made from all kinds of materials. They must build a nest that is strong and secure for their eggs and for the baby birds when they hatch.

What is different about the nests in the book? How is each one suited to the birds' environment and needs?

Have you seen a bird nest? What was it made of? Where did the bird make it?

· ·

MATERIALS

- [ ] Reusable resources such as shredded paper, pieces of string or yarn, toothpicks, and pipe cleaners
- [ ] Connectors such as wire, glue, and paste
- [ ] Tools such as scissors and pliers
- [ ] Natural items such as leaves, grass, twigs, mud, and branches
- [ ] A toy bird and plastic eggs
- [ ] Paper and markers, crayons, or pencils
- [ ] A bird nest to examine (optional)

TINKER WITH THE MATERIALS

Gather several items and explore them. What do you discover? What do you think you could make with the materials? What do you think a bird might do with them? Look for a way to hold the items together. What's another way?

STEM CONCEPTS

animal habitats / climate / environment / measurement / number concepts / properties of materials / scientific inquiry / structural engineering

A Sturdy Nest

THE DESIGN CHALLENGE

Making Build a strong bird nest.

Engineering Build a strong nest that will hold the most weight possible. It must be strong enough to hold three plastic eggs and a toy bird. It must sit on a branch without falling while holding the eggs and the toy bird.

WORKING ON THE DESIGN CHALLENGE

- **Think about it.** Look out of a window or go on a walk to watch the birds. Look closely at the bird nest in the classroom or at the pictures of the nests in the book. What materials did the birds use to build their nests? Where do you think they found the materials? What do you want to use to make your nest? Draw or sketch your ideas.

    Engineering. Select a picture of a bird and think about where it lives and the type of habitat it needs. Where is its nest located? Look at the materials that are available. How will you build your nest? What will you do to make it strong enough to hold the bird and the eggs?

- **Build or create it.** Choose materials to construct your nest. Make sure that it is strong and sturdy.

- **Try it.** Balance the nest on a firm surface.

    Engineering. Balance the nest on a branch. How many plastic eggs can you add? What happens when you add the toy bird?

- **Revise or make it better.** Does the nest stay in one piece? If it doesn't, what can you change to make it stronger?

    Engineering. Does your nest stay on the branch with at least three eggs and a toy bird inside it? If not, what can you change to make it stronger or more stable?

- **Share.** Write or dictate a story about a bird that might use your nest.

    Engineering. Explain to someone why you made the nest the way you did. Tell them what kind of bird might make this nest and why.

A Sturdy Nest

QUESTIONS AND COMMENTS

What do you think will happen if _____?

I wonder why your nest fell apart.

Would you want to use glue or tape to keep the nest together? Why or why not? What else could you use to hold it together?

How could you change your design so that it _____?

BACK TO THE PROBLEM IN THE BOOK

How does the nest you built compare with the nests in *Mama Built a Little Nest*? Do you think the baby birds would like the nest you built? Why or why not?

GOING DEEPER

- A bird doesn't have hands and fingers like you do to help it build its nest. How does it manipulate the materials? Try to build a nest like a bird would.

- Try weaving some of your items together.

- Would your nest stay together and balanced on a branch in the wind and rain? What could you do to make it strong enough to stand up against wind and rain?

OTHER BOOKS TO USE

Are You My Mother? / P.D. Eastman

The Best Nest / P.D. Eastman

Have You Heard the Nesting Bird? / Rita Gray, illustrated by Kenard Pak

Tower Power

Inspired by *Rapunzel*
by Sarah Gibb

Tower Power

LET'S LOOK AT THE PROBLEM

Rapunzel is a beautiful girl with long, golden hair. She is locked in a tower with no stairs or door, but visitors can climb up Rapunzel's hair to the top of the tower.

What could Rapunzel use to get people and objects up into the tower so they won't have to climb her hair?

* *

MATERIALS

☐ Reusable resources such as rubber bands, string, yarn, craft sticks, paper plates, paper cups, paper towel rolls, pipe cleaners, wooden skewers, and empty thread or ribbon spools

☐ Connectors such as tape, glue, brads, clothespins, cardboard connectors, wire, paper clips, twine, and Velcro

☐ Tools such as scissors, pulleys, measuring tapes, child-safe cardboard cutters, a low-temperature glue gun, and rulers

☐ Building materials for the tower such as blocks, boxes, Pringles cans, and oatmeal boxes

☐ Paper and markers, crayons, or pencils

Safety note: Adult assistance needed in cutting cardboard

TINKER WITH THE MATERIALS

Explore the materials and determine how you might move things from one place to another without picking them up or carrying them.

Investigate the pulley system on a flagpole. How does it work? Tinker with hauling items up and down with a pulley and a rope attached to a bucket or pail.

STEM CONCEPTS

balance / design engineering / geometric shapes / gravity / measurement / scientific inquiry / stability

Tower Power

THE DESIGN CHALLENGE

Making Use any materials to move objects from one place to another without touching or carrying them.

Engineering Rapunzel is tired of people using her hair to climb the tower to visit her or bring her things! Build a basket that can support weight and be lifted from the ground to the top of the tower using a pulley system.

WORKING ON THE DESIGN CHALLENGE

- **Think about it.** Look at the materials. What might you use to move things from one place to another? Talk about and draw or sketch your idea.

  Engineering. Think about the pulleys you have seen and how they work. What materials will you need to create your pulley system? What kind of container will you need to move the materials up to the top of the tower?

- **Build or create it.** Create a way to move an object without touching it with your hands or body.

  Engineering. How much string or rope will you need? How will you make it strong enough to carry the object? What will you use to create a pulley? Will you use one pulley or two?

- **Try it.** Were you able to move the object without using your hands or body?

  Engineering. Add weights to the container to see how much you can move.

- **Revise or make it better.** How did it work? What can you change to make it better?

  Engineering. What changes can you make so you can add more weight?

- **Share.** Share your creation with someone else. Show them which tools and materials you used to construct it. Ask them if they have any ideas about how to make it better.

  Engineering. Take photos of each phase of building your tower and pulley system. Create a slideshow or digital photo album showing your pulley system in action.

Tower Power

QUESTIONS AND COMMENTS

I wonder what would happen if _____.

Tell me how you made your pulley system.

I notice that when you pull down on the string, the container goes up. I wonder why.

What was most challenging when you were making your pulley system?

BACK TO THE PROBLEM IN THE BOOK

Would the pulley system you built be strong enough to carry the prince to the top of the tower to visit Rapunzel?

GOING DEEPER

- How could you use two pulleys in your design?
- Make a tower that is twice as tall as the one you built. How would your pulley system need to change?
- How could you use a small hobby motor and batteries to operate the pulley?

OTHER BOOKS TO USE

Gustave Eiffel's Spectacular Idea: The Eiffel Tower / Sharon Katz Cooper, illustrated by Janna Bock

Pull, Lift, and Lower: A Book About Pulleys / Michael Dahl, illustrated by Denise Shea

The Tree House That Jack Built / Bonnie Verburg, illustrated by Mark Teague

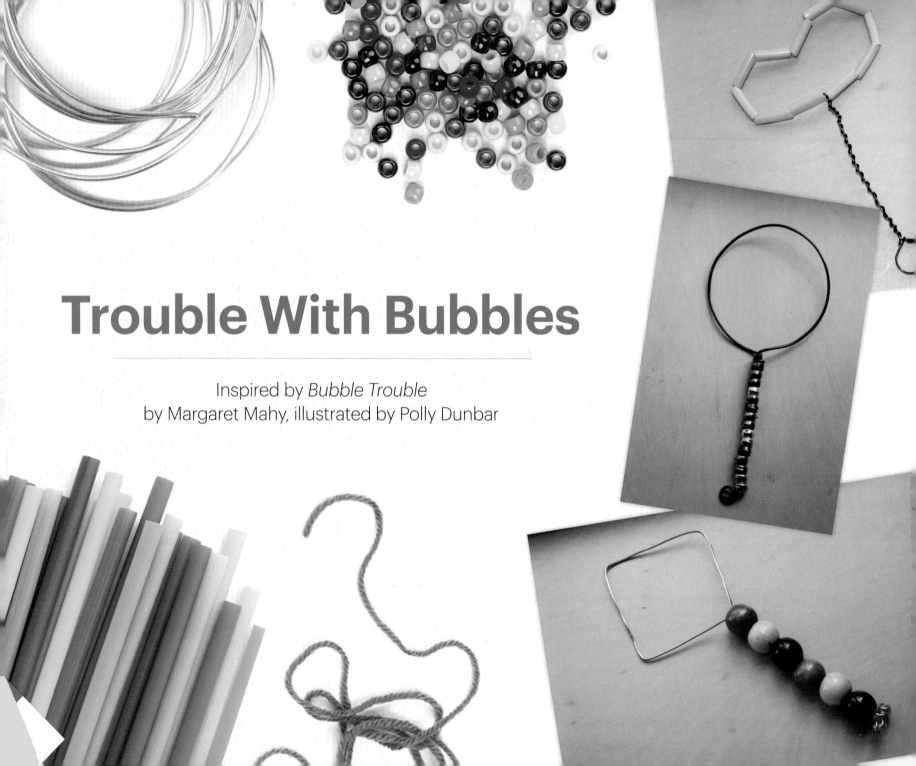

Trouble With Bubbles

Inspired by *Bubble Trouble*
by Margaret Mahy, illustrated by Polly Dunbar

Trouble With Bubbles

LET'S LOOK AT THE PROBLEM

One of Mabel's bubbles captures her baby brother. Off he floats, higher and higher above the town—with Mabel, Mother, and the whole town in pursuit!

How do the people plan to bring the baby safely down?

How does all the trouble start? What kind of bubble wand was Mabel was using? How could you make a wand for blowing bubbles?

. . . .

MATERIALS

- [ ] Reusable resources such as pipe cleaners, drinking straws, string, wire, berry baskets, paper cups, beads, and pipettes (special droppers for transporting specific amounts of liquid)
- [ ] Connectors such as tape
- [ ] Bubble solution (e.g., 2/3 cup liquid dish soap, 1 gallon water, and 2–3 tablespoons glycerin)
- [ ] Containers for the bubble solution such as trays or buckets
- [ ] A fan
- [ ] Paper and markers, crayons, or pencils

TINKER WITH THE MATERIALS

Experiment with blowing bubbles using several of the materials. What do you notice? What happens when you use a fan to blow the bubbles?

STEM CONCEPTS

chemistry / design engineering / elasticity / force / geometry / light / measurement / properties of liquids / scientific inquiry / spatial relationships / surface tension / tensile strength / wind

Trouble With Bubbles

THE DESIGN CHALLENGE

Making Make a bubble wand any way you choose.

Engineering Make bubble wands that are 3-D geometric shapes, like pyramids, cubes, rectangular prisms, or cylinders.

WORKING ON THE DESIGN CHALLENGE

- **Think about it.** Look at the different materials available. How will you make your wand? Will you use one type of material or a combination? Draw or sketch your idea.

    Engineering. What shape will you make your wand? Think about 3-D objects like a can, a box, or a pyramid-shaped block. How will you make a wand that is a similar shape?

- **Build or create it.** Use the materials to make your wand.

    Engineering. As you build your wand, look at a 3-D object like a can or a box. How many sides and corners does it have?

- **Try it.** Test out your wand with the bubble solution.

    Engineering. Lower your 3-D geometric wand slowly into a bucket of the bubble solution and pull it out gently. Do not blow on the wand yet. What shapes do

you see in the bubble? Jiggle the wand a bit and see what happens to the shapes. Now blow on the wand slowly. What happens?

- **Revise or make it better.** How does your wand work? What can you change to make it work better?

    Engineering. What shape are your bubbles when they are moving in the air? What shape are they when they are in your wand? Do you need to make any changes to your wand to improve the shapes?

- **Share.** Invite someone to try out your wand. What changes would they suggest?

    Engineering. Create a video or photos of bubbles made with wands of different shapes. Explain how you made them.

Trouble With Bubbles

QUESTIONS AND COMMENTS

I wonder what would happen if _____.

How does the shape of the wand change the shape of the bubble?

I wonder what makes bubbles pop.

How could you change your design so that it _____?

If a bubble is floating in the air and isn't in contact with any other object, what shape does it make?

BACK TO THE PROBLEM IN THE BOOK

How else could the people have helped the baby get down from his bubble?

Have you ever been in a tight spot you had to get out of? How did you do it? Did someone help you? What tools did you use?

How big do you think the bubble was to hold a baby? How could we figure that out?

If a bubble whisked you away, where would you like to go? How would you get down?

GOING DEEPER

- Make several wands of different materials and compare how well they work. What happens to the bubbles? How does the material of the wand affect the bubbles? Do some materials make better bubbles or bubbles that last longer? Why? What other factors might affect the bubbles?

- Create a wand that will blow more than one bubble at a time.

- Experiment with different ingredients to make a new bubble solution. What combinations make the longest-lasting bubbles? What else do you notice about the mixtures? How could you add some color?

- Create a bubble blower that will make bubbles larger than your head. What materials will you need?

- Design and create another type of bubble blower besides a wand.

OTHER BOOKS TO USE

Bubble Bubble / Mercer Mayer

The Bubble Factory / Tomie dePaola

Chavela and the Magic Bubble / Monica Brown, illustrated Magaly Morales

What a Car!

Inspired by *If I Built a Car*
by Chris Van Dusen

What a Car!

LET'S LOOK AT THE PROBLEM

While riding in the backseat of the family car, Jack tells his dad about the dream car he wants to build. It will have a snack bar, go underwater, drive on autopilot, fly, and do other totally amazing things.

Why does Jack want to build a new car? How will his car be both stylish and safe? Have you ever dreamed of having a car, a bike, or something else that could do cool things? Describe it.

• •

MATERIALS

- [ ] Reusable resources such as plastic bottles, bottle caps, paper towel tubes, cardboard, boxes, paper plates, foil pans, rubber bands, balloons, drinking straws, and craft sticks
- [ ] Connectors such as tape, glue, cardboard connectors, and brads
- [ ] Tools such as measuring tapes, rulers, paintbrushes, and child-size screwdrivers and hammers
- [ ] Pictures of different types of cars
- [ ] Old car parts such as mirrors, hubcaps, small motors, seatbelts, and radios
- [ ] Toy cars that can be disassembled
- [ ] Items for decorating such as paint, pom-poms, glitter, feathers, and googly eyes
- [ ] Paper and markers, crayons, or pencils

TINKER WITH THE MATERIALS

Investigate and tinker with real car parts. Use small screwdrivers to take them apart and put them back together. What did you discover?

Take an old toy car apart and find out how it works.

STEM CONCEPTS

geometry / measurement / mechanical engineering / number concepts / scientific inquiry / simple machines / speed / structural engineering

What a Car!

THE DESIGN CHALLENGE

Making   Build a car that can do something special.

Engineering   Build a car that has one or more special features and can travel two feet or more by itself.

WORKING ON THE DESIGN CHALLENGE

- **Think about it.** Look at the pictures of different types of cars. What parts do all cars have? How will you include these in your car? What special thing do you want your car to do? Draw or sketch your ideas. How will you build it to make that happen?

  Engineering. What will you use to make your car move on its own? Think about all the different things your car might do. Will you choose one special feature or more? Will your car drive on land, or also in the air (maybe in space) or water like Jack's?

- **Build or create it.** Gather your materials and build the car.

  Engineering. How will you make your car go on its own?

- **Try it.** Test your car and its special feature.

  Engineering. Does your car have all the special features that you wanted? Can it move on its own? How far does it go? How fast does it travel?

- **Revise or make it better.** What works and what doesn't? What can you change to make your car better?

  Engineering. How could you make your car go faster or farther?

- **Share.** Tell someone about your car and how you made it. Ask them if they have ideas about how to improve it. Or make up a simple rhyme or song that describes your car's features, like we read in *If I Built a Car*.

  Engineering. Write and illustrate an owner's manual that describes how to operate your car.

What a Car!

QUESTIONS AND COMMENTS

What did you think about when you designed your car?

What happens when you roll your car on different surfaces?

What tools could you use to _____?

What if I wanted to play some music in your car? How would I do that?

BACK TO THE PROBLEM IN THE BOOK

Jack's dream car has some pretty amazing features! Are any of them possible? A long time ago, cars didn't exist at all; people had to imagine what they wanted a car to do and look like and then figure out how to build it that way. Are any of your ideas for your car possible to design and make?

GOING DEEPER

- Imagine a character that has some special power or feature. Design a car that will help this character use that power. What would the car look like and do? Draw it and write about it, and then create it.

- Design and build a car that uses a battery and motor to move. How far do you think it can go? What other materials will you need?

OTHER BOOKS TO USE

Cars: Rushing! Honking! Zooming! / Patricia Hubbell, illustrated by Megan Halsey and Sean Addy

My Little Car / Gary Soto, illustrated by Pam Paparone

Otto: The Boy Who Loved Cars / Kara LaReau, illustrated by Scott Magoon

Wind Wonders

Inspired by *The Wind Blew*
by Pat Hutchins

Wind Wonders

LET'S LOOK AT THE PROBLEM

A problem arises on a day when the wind nearly blows an umbrella, a kite, a wig, and other items out to sea.

Has the wind ever blown your hat off your head? Why do you think the wind can be very strong?

• •

MATERIALS

- ☐ Reusable resources such as plastic cups, paper towel rolls, construction paper, cardboard, wood scraps, wooden spools, and corks
- ☐ Connectors such as tape, glue, pipe cleaners, and string
- ☐ Table tennis balls, pom-poms, and other lightweight materials to blow around
- ☐ Drinking straws
- ☐ Egg timers
- ☐ Paper and markers, crayons, or pencils

TINKER WITH THE MATERIALS

Blow through drinking straws to move table tennis balls, pom-poms, and other lightweight materials from one place to another. Which are easiest to move by blowing through a drinking straw?

STEM CONCEPTS

air / design engineering / force / friction / geometry / gravity / measurement / momentum / motion / scientific inquiry / wind

Wind Wonders

THE DESIGN CHALLENGE

Making   Use a drinking straw to blow a table tennis ball from one place to another.

Engineering   Construct a maze by taping obstacles on a tabletop. Blow air through a straw to move a table tennis ball through the maze.

WORKING ON THE DESIGN CHALLENGE

- **Think about it.** Do you think the ball will move faster on some surfaces (rug, tabletop, tile) than on others? Draw or sketch your ideas.

  Engineering. Look at the materials you have available. How will you create your maze?

- **Build or create it.** Set up the area where you will move the table tennis ball.

  Engineering. Construct your maze on a tabletop.

- **Try it.** Blow through a drinking straw to move the table tennis ball.

  Engineering. Using a drinking straw, move the table tennis ball through the maze without touching the ball.

- **Revise or make it better.** Are you able to move the ball? If not, what do you need to do so it works?

  Engineering. Are you able to move the ball through the maze? How can you make it better or more challenging?

- **Share.** Ask someone else to use a drinking straw to move the ball on the same surface. Is that person's experience the same as yours? Why or why not?

  Engineering. Share your maze with someone else and let them try it. Ask them what they would do differently. Challenge an opponent and see who can move the ball through the maze the fastest.

Wind Wonders

QUESTIONS AND COMMENTS

What other kinds of obstacles can you make in your maze?

How many seconds do you think it will take to move your ball through the maze?

What could you do to move the ball more quickly through the maze?

BACK TO THE PROBLEM IN THE BOOK

Do you think you would be able to move the objects that the author mentions in *The Wind Blew* by blowing through a drinking straw? Why or why not?

GOING DEEPER

- Use thicker, thinner, or longer straws to move the ball. Is it harder or easier?

- How far can you blow the ball? Is it the same distance each time? Make a graph that shows how far the ball goes each time.

- Is it easier to keep the ball moving or to let it stop after each time you blow through the drinking straw?

OTHER BOOKS TO USE

The Boy Who Harnessed the Wind: Picture Book Edition / William Kamkwamba and Bryan Mealer, illustrated by Elizabeth Zunon

Flora's Very Windy Day / Jeanne Birdsall, illustrated by Matt Phelan

I Face the Wind / Vicki Cobb, illustrated by Julia Gorton

Yarn Magic

Inspired by *Extra Yarn* by Mac Barnett,
illustrated by Jon Klassen

Yarn Magic

LET'S LOOK AT THE PROBLEM

Annabelle finds a box of extra yarn and knits sweaters for everyone in her town. She then knits sweaters for things like trees, buildings, and cars! She never runs out of yarn. When Annabelle finds a pile of sticks, she wonders what else she can create.

If you could cover something with yarn, what would it be?

• •

MATERIALS

- ☐ Natural items such as sticks, pinecones, leaves, flowers, and smaller and larger branches
- ☐ Connectors such as glue and tape
- ☐ Tools such as scissors, dull darning needles, mesh plastic canvases, and measuring tapes
- ☐ Yarn in a variety of colors, textures, and precut lengths
- ☐ Items for decorating such as fabric markers, pom-poms, feathers, glitter, beads, and googly eyes
- ☐ An old baby mobile to disassemble
- ☐ Paper and markers, crayons, or pencils

TINKER WITH THE MATERIALS

Feel the different textures of the yarn and examine the sticks. Can you create something with these materials? How can you hold things together? Think about which yarn you would use to wrap a stick.

Take apart an old baby mobile. How does it wind up? Does it play music? If so, how? How are the objects hung from the mobile?

STEM CONCEPTS

air movement / balance / geometry / gravity / measurement / scientific inquiry / structural engineering / symmetry / wind

Yarn Magic

THE DESIGN CHALLENGE

Making — Create a magic wand by wrapping yarn around a stick.

Engineering — Create a mobile using the magic wands (see Making, above) and other items from nature.

WORKING ON THE DESIGN CHALLENGE

- **Think about it.** Look at the sticks and yarn and decide what you will use. Predict how much yarn it will take to wrap your stick. Draw or sketch your ideas.

  Engineering. How many sticks will you need for your mobile? How much yarn do you think you will need? How will you balance your mobile? How and where will you hang it?

- **Build or create it.** Gather your materials and create your yarn wand. Is your prediction right about the amount of yarn it would take to wrap the stick?

  Engineering. Is your prediction right about how many sticks you would need to make a mobile?

- **Try it.** Decide what you want to use your magic wand for.

  Engineering. Test out your mobile. Is it balanced?

- **Revise or make it better.** How could you improve your magic wand?

  Engineering. If the mobile is not balanced, what can you change to make it balanced? What other items from nature could you add to your mobile? Remember to keep it balanced.

- **Share.** Tell someone how you made your magic wand.

  Engineering. Explain to someone the challenges you faced and resolved while making your mobile. Ask someone else what they would do differently or what other items they might use if they made a mobile.

Yarn Magic

QUESTIONS AND COMMENTS

I wonder how much yarn it will take to wrap the stick.

I wonder what would happen if _____.

This side of the mobile seems lower than that one. What will you change to make it balanced?

BACK TO THE PROBLEM IN THE BOOK

What other things could you wrap with yarn?

If your magic wand really worked, what would you want it to do?

GOING DEEPER

- Measure the amount of yarn it takes to wrap your stick. How much yarn do you think you would need to wrap a block? a book? a paintbrush?

- Create a mobile with sticks that are about the same size. Is it easy to balance the sticks in the mobile? Now create one with sticks that are different lengths and widths. Is it easier or harder to make a balanced mobile?

- Learn how to use yarn in a different way, such as weaving, crocheting, knitting, or embroidery.

- An art mobile is a type of *kinetic sculpture*—this means that it is artwork that has moving parts powered by the wind, a motor, or people. Research other types of kinetic sculptures and try creating one.

OTHER BOOKS TO USE

Just How Long Can a Long String Be?! / Keith Baker

Noodle's Knitting / Sheryl Webster, illustrated by Caroline Pedler

The Very Busy Spider / Eric Carle

Inspiring Children to Tinker, Make, and Engineer

As you can see, the experiences in this book are not a step-by-step set of instructions for you to complete with children. The challenges are just a starting point, and they are designed to spark a genuine love for tinkering, making, and engineering. Each design challenge can and should be shaped to meet the interests, needs, and abilities of the children you teach. As you implement the challenges in your program or classroom, children will be eager to investigate, ask questions, use their imaginations, and solve problems. Watching children truly engage in learning about the world around them, how things work, and how to make our world a better place for everyone is not only inspirational but important. We don't know what problems will confront children in the future, but the knowledge, skills, and dispositions they acquire through experiences such as these will help them become competent and confident problem solvers for tomorrow.

Appendix

Design Challenge Planning Template

Use this template as a planning tool to create design challenges to engage children in tinkering, making, and engineering experiences.

Identify a picture book in which the character(s) have a problem to solve.

Example: ***The Three Billy Goats Gruff*** by Paul Galdone

_____

_____

_____

_____

What materials do you think the children need to solve the problem?

Example: **Craft sticks, drinking straws, toothpicks, paper, newspaper, straw, clay, paper clips, tape, scissors, glue, measuring tapes, and a balance scale**

_____

_____

_____

_____

What is the problem in the story?

Example: **Three billy goats want to go up a hillside to eat some grass. But they have to cross a bridge to get there, and under the bridge lives a mean, ugly old troll who wants to eat them.**

_____

_____

_____

How could you encourage children to tinker with the materials?

Example: **Tinker with making bridges out of materials like craft sticks, toothpicks, straws, paper, rolled-up newspaper, or clay. How will you hold the materials together? Which materials seem stronger than others?**

_____

_____

_____

What is the challenge for children?

Example:

Making. Build a troll-proof bridge that stands on its own so the goats can cross the river.

Engineering. Build a troll-proof bridge that spans at least 10 inches and supports at least five pounds.

_____

_____

Individualize these steps to reflect the book you've selected and the problem that needs to be solved. For ideas, see "What You Need to Know About Tinkering, Making, and Engineering" on pages 1–19.

Step 1: Think about it. Example: You may want to draw or sketch your plan before you begin.

_____

_____

Step 2: Build or create it. Example: Use the materials to build or construct the solution to your problem.

_____

_____

Step 3: Try it. Example: How can you test your idea? Does it do what you want it to do?

_____

_____

Step 4: Revise or make it better. Example: What could you do or change to make it better?

_____

_____

Step 5: Share. Example: Show your project to other people and demonstrate how it works. Ask them what they might do to solve the problem. Listen to their ideas.

_____

_____

What questions or comments might you use to scaffold the children's ideas?

_____

_____

What additional challenges might help children think more deeply about the problem?

_____

_____

Which STEM concepts are supported by the design challenge?

_____

_____

Books and Materials for Design Challenges

Design Challenge	Book Suggestions	Materials Other Than Reusable Resources, Connectors, and Tools
Baby Bear's Chair	*Goldilocks and the Three Bears* *A Chair for Baby Bear* *A Chair for My Mother* *Peter's Chair*	Broken or nonworking toys or small appliances Scale and 5 lb. weight
Beautiful Buildings	*Iggy Peck, Architect* *Dreaming Up: A Celebration of Building* *First Shapes in Buildings* *How a House Is Built*	Photos of tall buildings 100 pennies
Box It!	*Not a Box* *A Box Story* *Clancy and Millie and the Very Fine House* *What to Do With a Box*	Items for decorating
Bug City	*Roberto: The Insect Architect* *The Best Book of Bugs* *A House Is a House for Me* *Insects and Spiders*	Building toys Nonfiction books and videos about insects Blueprints and graph paper Small toy insects 8 oz. weight
Build a Bridge	*The Three Billy Goats Gruff* *Pop's Bridge* *This Bridge Will Not Be Gray* *Twenty-One Elephants and Still Standing*	Photos of bridges Scale and three 5 lb. weights

Design Challenge	Book Suggestions	Materials Other Than Reusable Resources, Connectors, and Tools
Crazy Catapults	*Olympig!* *Explore Simple Machines! With 25 Great Projects* *The Knight and the Dragon* *Simon and Catapult Man's Perilous Playground Adventure*	Small, lightweight objects (pom-poms, cotton balls, etc.) Photos of catapults
Float Your Boat	*Who Sank the Boat?* *The Gingerbread Boy* *Mr. Gumpy's Outing* *Toy Boat*	Pennies, packing peanuts, bottle caps, or other weights Large container of water
Gizmos Galore	*Rosie Revere, Engineer* *Papa's Mechanical Fish* *Violet the Pilot* *What Do You Do With an Idea?*	Everyday objects (backpack, toothbrush, piggy bank, etc.) Toys to take apart that have moving parts
Help! It's Stuck!	*Stuck* *Bubble Gum, Bubble Gum* *My Truck Is Stuck!* *Tikki Tikki Tembo*	Small, lightweight objects to suspend Photos of (or objects with) scissor linkages
A House for the Three Little Pigs	*The Three Little Pigs* *The Three Horrid Little Pigs* *The Three Little Pigs: An Architectural Tale* *The True Story of the 3 Little Pigs!*	Toys for building (LEGO bricks, blocks, small building planks, etc.) Fan or other wind-making device

Design Challenge	Book Suggestions	Materials Other Than Reusable Resources, Connectors, and Tools
If the Shoe Fits	*The Elves and the Shoemaker* *Pete the Cat: I Love My White Shoes* *Shoes for Me!* *Shoes, Shoes, Shoes*	Variety of old shoes Items for decorating Old sneaker cut to show layers (optional)
Juice It!	*Caterina and the Lemonade Stand* *Lemonade for Sale* *Lemonade in Winter: A Book About Two Kids Counting Money* *Once Upon a Company...: A True Story*	Juicing gadgets and sealable sandwich bags Kitchen utensils (cups, bowls, measuring spoons) Fruits
Move Like an Animal	*Fraidyzoo* *Put Me in the Zoo* *A Sick Day for Amos McGee* *What If You Had...!? (series)*	Items for decorating Picture books, photos, or videos of animals
Paper Airplanes	*The Great Paper Caper* *Float* *Kids' Paper Airplane Book* *Whoosh! Easy Paper Airplanes for Kids: Color, Fold, and Fly!*	Paper clips and brads to use as weights
Pet Carrier	*A Home for Dixie: The True Story of a Rescued Puppy* *Before You Were Mine* *A Home for Dakota* *Yoda: The Story of a Cat and His Kittens*	Scale and a 5 lb. weight Pet toys, blankets, and water bowls

Design Challenge	Book Suggestions	Materials Other Than Reusable Resources, Connectors, and Tools
Repurpose It!	*The Most Magnificent Thing* *Awesome Dawson* *The Branch* *Choose to Reuse*	Old toys to take apart (toy car, cash register, etc.)
Roller Coaster	*Roller Coaster* *Curious George Roller Coaster* *Harriet and the Roller Coaster* *The Roller Coaster Kid*	Small balls or marbles Stopwatch
Squirrel-Proof Birdfeeder	*Those Darn Squirrels!* *Nuts to You!* *The Secret Life of Squirrels* *The Tale of Squirrel Nutkin*	Items for decorating
Strike Up the Band	*Olivia Forms a Band* *Ah, Music!* *Max Found Two Sticks* *Tito Puente: Mambo King/Rey del Mambo*	Items for decorating Musical instruments
A Sturdy Nest	*Mama Built a Little Nest* *Are You My Mother?* *The Best Nest* *Have You Heard the Nesting Bird?*	Natural items (twigs, branches, leaves, etc.) Toy bird and plastic eggs Bird nest (optional)

Design Challenge	Book Suggestions	Materials Other Than Reusable Resources, Connectors, and Tools
Tower Power	*Rapunzel* *Gustave Eiffel's Spectacular Idea: The Eiffel Tower* *Pull, Lift, and Lower: A Book About Pulleys* *The Tree House That Jack Built*	Building materials (blocks, boxes, Pringles cans, etc.)
Trouble With Bubbles	*Bubble Trouble* *Bubble Bubble* *The Bubble Factory* *Chavela and the Magic Bubble*	Bubble solution (dish soap, water, and glycerin) Trays and buckets Fan
What a Car!	*If I Built a Car* *Cars: Rushing! Honking! Zooming!* *My Little Car* *Otto: The Boy Who Loved Cars*	Pictures of different cars Old car parts (mirrors, hubcaps, etc.) Toy cars to take apart Items for decorating
Wind Wonders	*The Wind Blew* *The Boy Who Harnessed the Wind: Picture Book Edition* *Flora's Very Windy Day* *I Face the Wind*	Table tennis balls and pom-poms Drinking straws Egg timers
Yarn Magic	*Extra Yarn* *Just How Long Can a Long String Be?!* *Noodle's Knitting* *The Very Busy Spider*	Items for decorating Natural items (sticks, pinecones, leaves, etc.) Yarn Mobile to take apart

Book List

Ah, Music! 2003. Aliki. New York: HarperCollins.

Are You My Mother? 1960. P.D. Eastman. New York: Beginner Books.

Awesome Dawson. 2013. C. Gall. New York: Little, Brown and Company.

Before You Were Mine. 2007. M. Boelts. Illus. D. Walker. New York: G.P. Putnam's Sons.

The Best Book of Bugs. 1998. C. Llewellyn. Illus. C. Forsey, A.R. di Gaudesi, & D. Wright. New York: Kingfisher.

The Best Nest. 1968. P.D. Eastman. New York: Beginner Books.

A Box Story. 2012. K.K. Lamug. Las Vegas: RabbleBox.

The Boy Who Harnessed the Wind: Picture Book Edition. 2012. W. Kamkwamba & B. Mealer. Illus. E. Zunon. New York: Dial Books for Young Readers.

The Branch. 2016. M. Messier. Illus. P. Pratt. Toronto: Kids Can Press.

Bubble Bubble. 1973. M. Mayer. New York: Parents Magazine Press.

The Bubble Factory. 1996. T. dePaola. New York: Grosset & Dunlap.

Bubble Gum, Bubble Gum. 2004. L. Wheeler. Illus. L. Huliska-Beith. New York: Little, Brown and Company.

Bubble Trouble. 2008. M. Mahy. Illus. P. Dunbar. London: Frances Lincoln Limited Publishers.

Cars: Rushing! Honking! Zooming! 2006. P. Hubbell. Illus. M. Halsey & S. Addy. Tarrytown, NY: Marshall Cavendish Children.

Caterina and the Lemonade Stand. 2014. E.E. Kono. New York: Dial Books for Young Readers.

A Chair for Baby Bear. 2004. K. Umansky. Illus. C. Fisher. New York: Oxford University Press.

A Chair for My Mother. 1982. V.B. Williams. New York: Greenwillow Books.

Chavela and the Magic Bubble. 2010. M. Brown. Illus. M. Morales. New York: Clarion Books.

Choose to Reuse. 2011. L. Bullard. Illus. W. Thomas. Minneapolis: Millbrook Press.

Clancy and Millie and the Very Fine House. 2009. L. Gleeson. Illus. F. Blackwood. Sydney: Little Hare Books.

Curious George Roller Coaster. 2007. H.A. Rey & M. Perez. New York: Houghton Mifflin Company.

Dreaming Up: A Celebration of Building. 1996. C. Hale. New York: Lee & Low Books.

The Elves and the Shoemaker. 2003. J. LaMarche. San Francisco: Chronicle Books.

Explore Simple Machines! With 25 Great Projects. 2011. A. Yasuda. Illus. B. Stone. White River Junction, VT: Nomad Press.

Extra Yarn. 2012. M. Barnett. Illus. J. Klassen. New York: Balzer & Bray.

First Shapes in Buildings. 2009. P.A. Lane. London: Frances Lincoln Children's Books.

Float. 2015. D. Miyares. New York: Simon & Schuster Books for Young Readers.

Flora's Very Windy Day. 2010. J. Birdsall. Illus. M. Phelan. New York: Clarion Books.

Fraidyzoo. 2013. T. Heder. New York: Abrams Books for Young Readers.

The Gingerbread Boy. 1975. P. Galdone. New York: Seabury Press.

Goldilocks and the Three Bears. 2007. C. Buehner. Illus. M. Buehner. New York: Dial Books for Young Readers.

The Great Paper Caper. 2008. O. Jeffers. New York: Philomel Books.

Gustave Eiffel's Spectacular Idea: The Eiffel Tower. 2016. S.K. Cooper. Illus. J. Bock. Minneapolis: Picture Window Books.

Harriet and the Roller Coaster. 1982. N. Carlson. Minneapolis: Carolrhoda Books.

Have You Heard the Nesting Bird? 2014. R. Gray. Illus. K. Pak. New York: Houghton Mifflin Harcourt.

A Home for Dakota. 2008. J.Z. Grover. Illus. N. Lane. Edina, MN: The Gryphon Press.

A Home for Dixie: The True Story of a Rescued Puppy. 2008. E. Jackson. Photog. B. Carey. New York: Collins.

A House Is a House for Me. 1978. M.A. Hoberman. Illus. B. Fraser. New York: Viking Penguin.

How a House Is Built. 1990. G. Gibbons. New York: Holiday House.

I Face the Wind. 2003. V. Cobb. Illus. J. Gorton. New York: HarperCollins.

If I Built a Car. 2005. C. Van Dusen. New York: Dutton Children's Books.

Iggy Peck, Architect. 2007. A. Beaty. Illus. D. Roberts. New York: Abrams Books for Young Readers.

Insects and Spiders. 2015. B. Rin. Illus. D. Gam. Ed. J. Cowley. Strathfield, NSW, Australia: Big & Small.

Just How Long Can a Long String Be?! 2009. K. Baker. New York: Arthur A. Levine Books.

Kids' Paper Airplane Book. 1996. K. Blackburn & J. Lammers. New York: Workman Publishing Company.

The Knight and the Dragon. 1980. T. dePaola. New York: G.P. Putnam's Sons.

Lemonade for Sale. 1997. S.J. Murphy. Illus. T. Tusa. New York: HarperCollins.

Lemonade in Winter: A Book About Two Kids Counting Money. 2012. E. Jenkins. Illus. G.B. Karas. New York: Schwartz & Wade Books.

Mama Built a Little Nest. 2014. J. Ward. Illus. S. Jenkins. San Diego: Beach Lane Books.

Max Found Two Sticks. 1994. B. Pinkney. New York: Simon & Schuster Books for Young Readers.

The Most Magnificent Thing. 2014. A. Spires. Toronto: Kids Can Press.

Mr. Gumpy's Outing. 1970. J. Burningham. London: Jonathan Cape.

My Little Car. 2006. G. Soto. Illus. P. Paparone. New York: G.P. Putnam's Sons.

My Truck Is Stuck! 2002. K. Lewis. Illus. D. Kirk. New York: Hyperion Books for Children.

Noodle's Knitting. 2010. S. Webster. Illus. C. Pedler. Brattleboro, VT: Good Books.

Not a Box. 2006. A. Portis. New York: HarperCollins Children's Books.

Nuts to You! 1993. L. Ehlert. San Diego: Harcourt, Inc.

Olivia Forms a Band. 2006. I. Falconer. New York: Atheneum Books for Young Readers.

Olympig! 2012. V. Jamieson. New York: Dial Books for Young Readers.

Once Upon a Company...: A True Story. 1998. W.A. Halperin. New York: Orchard Books.

Otto: The Boy Who Loved Cars. 2011. K. LaReau. Illus. S. Magoon. New York: Roaring Brook Press.

Papa's Mechanical Fish. 2013. C. Fleming. Illus. B. Kulikov. New York: Farrar Straus Giroux Books for Young Readers.

Pete the Cat: I Love My White Shoes. 2010. E. Litwin. Illus. J. Dean. New York: HarperCollins Children's Books.

Peter's Chair. 1967. E.J. Keats. New York: Harper & Row.

Pop's Bridge. 2006. E. Bunting. Illus. C.F. Payne. Orlando: Harcourt, Inc.

Pull, Lift, and Lower: A Book About Pulleys. 2006. M. Dahl. Illus. D. Shea. Minneapolis: Picture Window Books.

Put Me in the Zoo. 1960. R. Lopshire. New York: Beginner Books.

Rapunzel. 2010. S. Gibb. New York: HarperCollins Children's Books.

Roberto: The Insect Architect. 2000. N. Laden. San Francisco: Chronicle Books.

Roller Coaster. 2003. M. Frazee. Orlando: Harcourt, Inc.

The Roller Coaster Kid. 2012. M.A. Rodman. Illus. R. Roth. New York: Viking.

Rosie Revere, Engineer. 2013. A. Beaty. Illus. D. Roberts. New York: Abrams Books for Young Readers.

The Secret Life of Squirrels. 2014. N. Rose. New York: Little, Brown and Company.

Shoes for Me! 2011. S. Fliess. Illus. M. Laughead. Tarrytown, NY: Marshall Cavendish Children.

Shoes, Shoes, Shoes. 1995. A. Morris. New York: Lothrop, Lee & Shepard Books.

A Sick Day for Amos McGee. 2010. P.C. Stead. Illus. E.E. Stead. New York: Roaring Brook Press.

Simon and Catapult Man's Perilous Playground Adventure. 2009. N. Smiley. Illus. B. Jones. Halifax, NS: Nimbus Publishing.

Stuck. 2011. O. Jeffers. New York: Philomel Books.

The Tale of Squirrel Nutkin. 1903. B. Potter. London: Frederick Warne & Co.

This Bridge Will Not Be Gray. 2015. D. Eggers. Illus. T. Nichols. San Francisco: McSweeney's.

Those Darn Squirrels! 2008. A. Rubin. Illus. D. Salmieri. New York: Clarion Books.

The Three Billy Goats Gruff. 1979. P. Galdone. New York: Seabury Press.

The Three Horrid Little Pigs. 2008. L. Pichon. Wilton, CT: Tiger Tales.

The Three Little Pigs. 1970. P. Galdone. New York: Seabury Press.

The Three Little Pigs: An Architectural Tale. 2010. S. Guarnaccia. New York: Abrams Books for Young Readers

Tikki Tikki Tembo. 1968. A. Mosel. Illus. B. Lent. New York: Henry Holt and Company.

Tito Puente: Mambo King/Rey del Mambo. Bilingual ed. 2013. M. Brown. Illus. R. López. New York: Rayo.

Toy Boat. 2007. R. de Sève. Illus. L. Long. New York: Philomel Books.

The Tree House That Jack Built. 2014. B. Verburg. Illus. M. Teague. New York: Orchard Books.

The True Story of the 3 Little Pigs! 1989. J. Scieszka. Illus. L. Smith. New York: Viking Penguin.

Twenty-One Elephants and Still Standing. 2005. A.J. Prince. Illus. F. Roca. Boston: HMH Books for Young Readers.

The Very Busy Spider. 1984. E. Carle. New York: Philomel Books.

Violet the Pilot. 2008. S. Breen. New York: Dial Books for Young Readers.

What Do You Do With an Idea? 2014. K. Yamada. Illus. M. Besom. Seattle: Compendium, Inc.

What If You Had...!? Series. 2012–16. S. Markle. Illus. H. McWilliam. New York: Scholastic.

What to Do With a Box. 2016. J. Yolen. Illus. C. Sheban. Mankato, MN: Creative Editions.

Who Sank the Boat? 1982. P. Allen. Edinburgh: Thomas Nelson.

Whoosh! Easy Paper Airplanes for Kids: Color, Fold, and Fly! 2013. A. Naylor. Illus. K. Schwede. Mineola, NY: Dover Publications.

The Wind Blew. 1974. P. Hutchins. New York: Macmillan Publishing Company.

Yoda: The Story of a Cat and His Kittens. 2014. B. Stern. Illus. D. Crane. New York: Aladdin.

About the Author

Cate Heroman's passion is to help children be successful learners and socially competent individuals. A nationally recognized educator and author—her numerous publications include *The Creative Curriculum for Preschool* and *Teaching Strategies GOLD*—Cate's professional experiences center on early childhood education. She has been an early childhood classroom teacher, state administrator, trainer, facilitator, keynote speaker, author, consultant, and developer of curriculum and assessment materials. She has a deep understanding not only of *what* children learn but also *how* they learn.

Cate is giving back to her community through her volunteer efforts with Knock Knock Children's Museum in Baton Rouge, Louisiana, serving children birth to age eight. She has been instrumental in establishing a makerspace in the museum and has spent countless hours studying and researching what making, tinkering, and design engineering look like with young learners. While much of the information available on these topics is for older students and adults, practical guidance for early childhood educators is limited. This book began as a tool for museum educators. During the field testing and piloting of the activities, however, Cate discovered a clear demand for this type of resource for educators in preschool through third grade classrooms.

Cate received a master's degree from Louisiana State University, taught in East Baton Rouge Parish Schools, served as an early childhood administrator at the Louisiana Department of Education, and was vice president of Teaching Strategies, LLC. She is education chair and vice chair of Knock Knock Children's Museum in Baton Rouge. She is married with two children and four grandchildren.

Acknowledgments

The foundation for this body of work began as a partnership between Knock Knock Children's Museum and Louisiana State University (LSU). A group came together in 2014 to brainstorm ideas for establishing a makerspace in the museum, located a mile from the university. In the planning phases of the museum, the group decided the museum should develop a series of engineering design challenges that would be piloted and tested before implementing them. The committee of experts reviewing and providing feedback on the design challenges were Dr. Frank Neubrander, Dr. Brenda Nixon, and Nell McAnelly from the LSU Gordon A. Cain Center for Scientific, Technological, Engineering, and Mathematical Literacy; Dr. Renee Casbergue, Dr. Cynthia DiCarlo, and Dr. Jennifer Baumgartner from the LSU College of Human Sciences and Education; and Kim Fossey, founder and leader of STEMup Baton Rouge. A special thanks to Dr. Baumgartner, who integrated the revised design challenges into her coursework, and to the LSU pre-K–3 students, who piloted the challenges and provided valuable feedback as part of their student teacher placement.

The Knock Knock Maker Shop committee, a group of educators and parents volunteering for the museum and shaping of the makerspace, includes Paige Zittrauer, Cathy Rosenfeld, Ni'Shawn Stovall, and Kelly Wood. These individuals provided ideas, suggestions, feedback, and inspiration during the development of this resource.

I am very grateful to former colleague Toni Bickart for her review, suggestions, and reflection. Thanks also to Ann Scalley, a preschool teacher at Lesley Ellis School in Arlington, Massachusetts, for her practical wisdom and creative ideas for many of the design challenges.

I am indebted to Ryan and Jackie Moreno, the administrators of the Play Make Share Program, a makerspace at REM Learning Center in Miami, Florida. My visits to their program underscored the value of tinkering and learning using real tools and technologies in early childhood. Their work helped solidify my thinking about the relationship of engineering design challenges to making and tinkering.

Many thanks to the teachers and children whose photographs and creations appear in the book:

- Kerry Sheldon and Sarah West's class, Louisiana State University Early Childhood Education Laboratory Preschool

- Paige Zittrauer's kindergarten class, Louisiana State University Laboratory School

- William Bronaugh, Julia Collick, Sydney Collick, August Huff, Juliana Huff, Amelia Matten, Fiona Matten, Isaac Matten, Aidan Stowell, and my grandchildren Lucy Bea Wood, John Isaac Wood, and Samantha Heroman

And finally, thank you to Kathy Charner, Susan Friedman, and the entire team at NAEYC for their support of early STEM education and their role in developing resources to help educators succeed in their work.